About Skill B

Geometry

Grades 6–8

by Douglas M. Sept

Welcome to the Skill Builders series. This series is designed to make learning both fun and rewarding.

Skill Builders *Geometry* provides students with focused practice to help them reinforce and develop geometry and math skills. This book provides grade-level-appropriate activities and clear instructions. The exercises cover a variety of geometry and math skills, including the Pythagorean theorem, pi, area and perimeter, and naming, measuring, and classifying angles. Skill Builders *Geometry* also includes an assessment section designed to help identify areas in which students need extra practice and instruction.

Learning is more effective when approached with enthusiasm. That's why the Skill Builders series combines academically sound exercises with engaging graphics and exciting themes—to make reviewing basic skills at school or at home fun and effective.

Credits:
Editor: Julie Kirsch
Layout Design: Mark Conrad
Cover Concept: Chasity Rice

www.summerbridgeactivities.com

 ISBN: 978-1-60022-145-3

Table of Contents

Formulas 3
Assessment Test 4
Along the Lines 8
Linear Relationships 9
Congruent Segments and Segment Addition 10
Midpoints 11
Naming, Measuring, and Classifying Angles 12
Congruent Angles and Angle Addition 13
Angle Bisectors 14
Complementary and Supplementary Angles 15
Vertical Angles 16
Corresponding Angles 17
Alternate Interior and Exterior Angles 18
Same-Side Interior Angles 19
Classifying Polygons 20
Polygon Angle Measures 21
Regular and Irregular Polygons 22
Drawing Polygons 23
Congruent Polygons 24
Classifying Triangles 25
Triangle Sum Theorem 26
Angle Measures of Triangles 27
Angle Puzzle 28
Congruent Triangles 29
Parts of Congruent Triangles 31
The Pythagorean Theorem 32
Applying the Pythagorean Theorem . . . 33
The Converse of the Pythagorean Theorem 34
Classifying Quadrilaterals 35
Angle Measures of Quadrilaterals 36
Side Lengths of Quadrilaterals 37
Solving Proportions 38
Similar Polygons 39
Similar Triangles 40
Applying Similarity 41
Solving Perimeter Problems 43
Area of Quadrilaterals 44
Area of Triangles and Trapezoids 45
Area of Irregular Shapes 46
Area of a Shaded Region 47
Proportional Perimeter and Area 48
Parts of Circles 49
Discovering Pi 50
Circumference 51
Area of Circles 52
Classifying Solids 53
Drawing Solids 54
Parts of a Prism 55
Viewing Solids from Different Perspectives 56
Nets 58
Surface Area of a Prism 59
Volume of a Prism 60
Surface Area of a Cylinder 61
Volume of a Cylinder 62
Surface Area Practice 63
Volume Practice 64
Volume of a Sphere 65
Identifying Transformations 66
Drawing Transformations 67
Symmetry 68
Identifying Points in a Coordinate Plane 69
Plotting Points in a Coordinate Plane . . . 70
Coordinate Translations 71
Coordinate Reflections 72
Coordinate Rotations 73
Coordinate Dilations 74
The Midpoint Formula 75
The Distance Formula 76
Answer Key 77

Formulas

Solving math problems can be easy if you know some common mathematical formulas. Study the formulas below and use this page as a reference as you work through this book.

Abbreviations

pi = π = 3.14	r = radius	w = width	d = diameter
l = length	h = height	b = base	$\angle$ = angle

Area

of a circle: πr^2

of a square: w^2

of a rectangle: lw

of a triangle: $\frac{1}{2}(bh)$

Surface Area

of a cylinder: $2\pi(r^2 + rh)$, or $2(\pi r^2) + 2(\pi rh)$

of a cube: $6w^2$

of a sphere: $4\pi r^2$

of a rectangular prism: $2(ab + ac + bc)$; a, b, and c are the lengths of the 3 sides

Volume

of a cube: w^3

of a cylinder: $\pi r^2 h$

of a rectangular prism: lwh

of a cone: $\frac{1}{3}\pi r^2 h$

of a pyramid: $\frac{1}{3}$ (bh)

of a sphere: $\frac{4}{3}\pi r^3$

Perimeter

of a circle: πd or $2\pi r$

of a square: 4w

of a rectangle: $2(a + b)$

of a triangle: $a + b + c$

Circumference

When given the diameter of a circle: πd

When given the radius of a circle: $2\pi r$

Pythagorean Theorem: $a^2 + b^2 = c^2$

Assessment Test

1. Find the volume and surface area for the solid below.

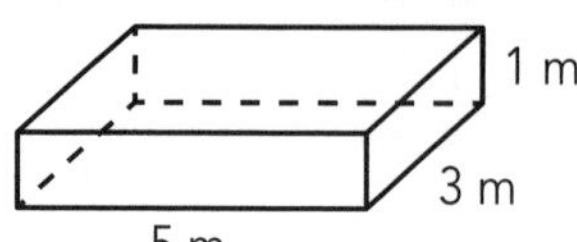

volume = ____________

surface area = ____________

2. The two legs of an isosceles trapezoid are congruent. Find the missing side lengths for isosceles trapezoid DEFG.

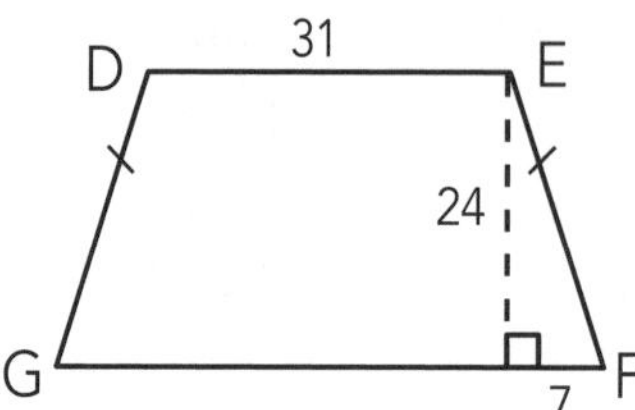

$\overline{DG}$ = _____

$\overline{GF}$ = _____

3. Identify each of the following linear parts.

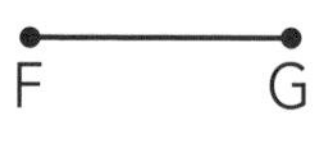

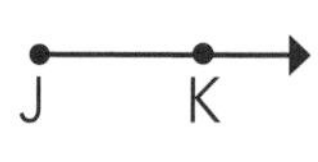

__________ __________ __________

4. Find the area and perimeter of the following triangle.

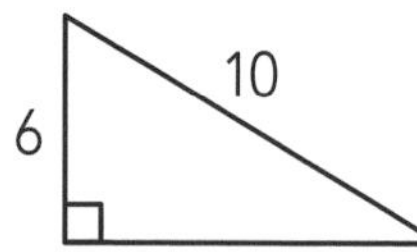

area = ____________

perimeter = ____________

5. Point D is the midpoint of $\overline{CE}$. Find the values.

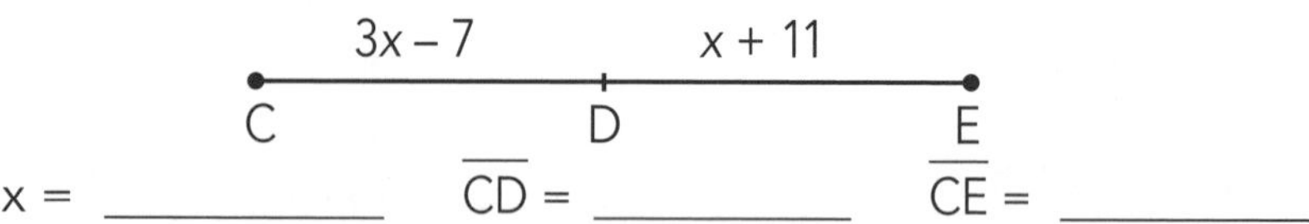

x = __________ $\overline{CD}$ = __________ $\overline{CE}$ = __________

6. Find the volume and surface area of the cylinder below.

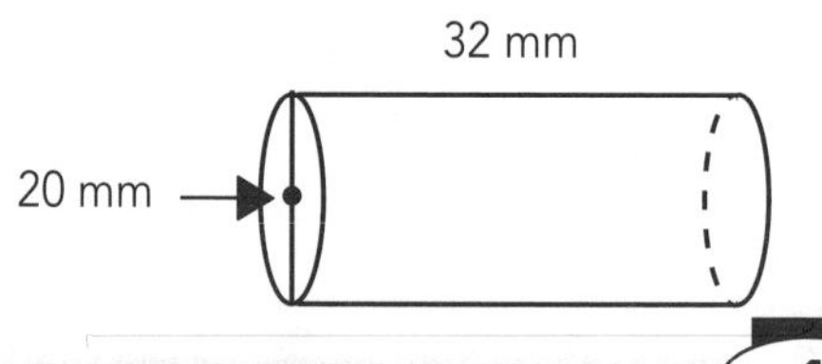

volume = ____________

surface area = ____________

7. Translate $\overline{AB}$ to the right 4 units and down 1 unit. Give the coordinates of the image points.

A' (_____ , _____)

B' (_____ , _____)

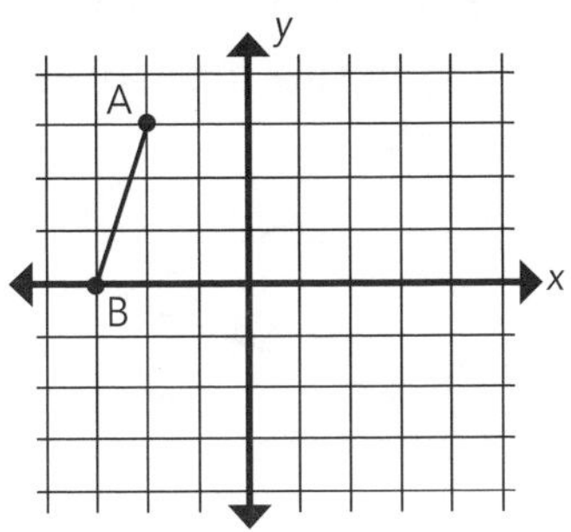

8. At 10:00 A.M., a 4' tall pole casts a 3' shadow. Determine the height of a building that casts a 60' shadow at the same time.

____

9. Find the missing angle measure. Then, classify each angle as acute, right, or obtuse.

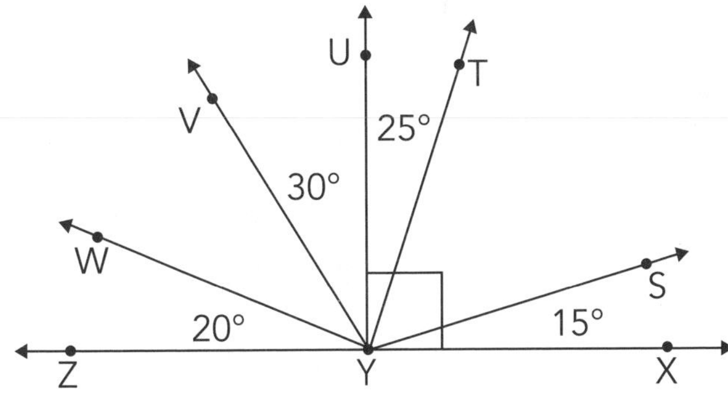

∠TYS = __________ ° ∠WYV = __________ ° ∠VYX = __________ °

__________ __________ __________

10. A circle has a diameter of 14 cm. Find the circumference of the circle. Then, find the area of the circle.

circumference = __________ area = __________

Assessment Test, continued

11. The interior angles of a quadrilateral equal 360°. Find the missing angle measures for quadrilateral GHIJ.

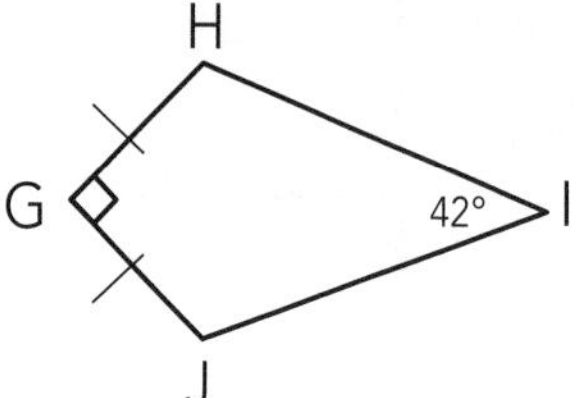

m∠H = ______________°

m∠J = ______________°

12. The interior angles of a triangle measure 180°. Find the missing angle measure.

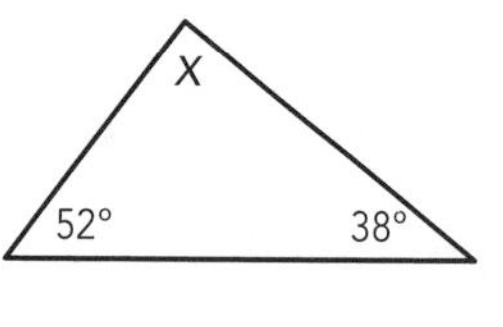

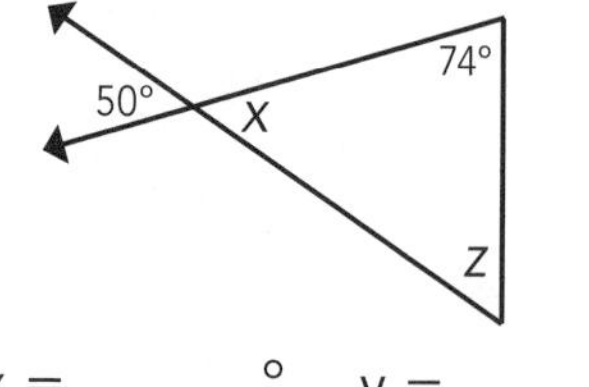

x = ______________°

x = _____° y = _____°

13. Reflect ΔDEF over the *x*-axis. Give the coordinates of the image points.

D' (_____ , _____)

E' (_____ , _____)

F' (_____ , _____)

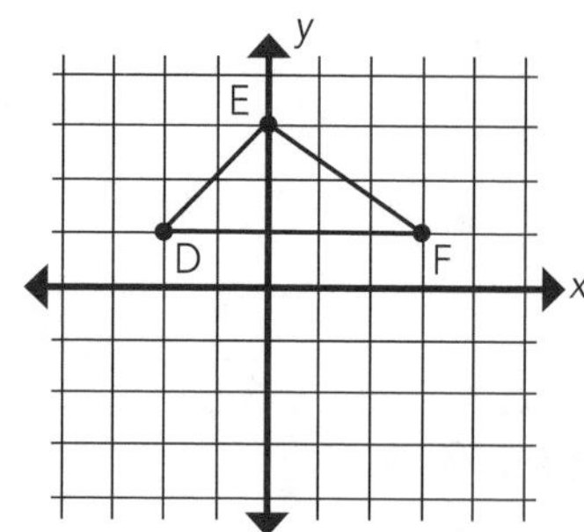

14. Draw the image that would be created after the given transformation.

translation right

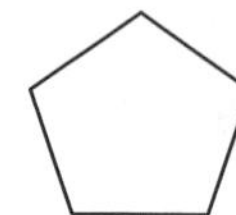

180° rotation about point K

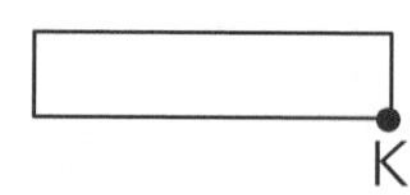

15. Find the sums of the measures of the interior angles for the following polygons. Use the formula S = (n – 2) • 180°.

hexagon = ______________ octagon = ______________

Assessment Test, continued

Check answers using the answer key provided (page 77). Match those problems with incorrect answers to the sections below. To ensure extra practice in problem areas, refer to the pages listed under each section.

Angles
Questions: 9, 11, 12
Review pages: 12–19

Area
Question: 4, 10
Review pages: 44–48

Circles
Question: 10
Review pages: 49–52

Coordinate Geometry
Questions: 7, 13
Review pages: 69–76

Linear Parts
Questions: 3, 5
Review pages: 8–11

Perimeter
Question: 4
Review pages: 43, 48

Pi
Questions: 6, 10
Review page: 50

Polygons
Question: 15
Review pages: 20–24

Pythagorean Theorem
Questions: 2, 4
Review pages: 32–34

Quadrilaterals
Questions: 2, 11
Review pages: 35–37

Similarity
Question: 8
Review pages: 38–42

Solids
Questions: 1, 6
Review pages: 53–65

Transformations
Questions: 7, 13, 14
Review pages: 66–67

Triangles
Questions: 4, 8, 12
Review pages: 25–34

Along the Lines

Linear Parts

A **point** is a location in space. • A — Point A

A **line** is a set of points that extend infinitely in two directions. A B — $\overleftrightarrow{AB}$ or $\overleftrightarrow{BA}$

A **ray** is part of a line with one endpoint. C D E — $\overrightarrow{DE}$ or $\overrightarrow{CE}$

A **segment** is part of a line with two endpoints. F G — $\overline{FG}$ or $\overline{GF}$

A **plane** is a set of points that extend infinitely in two dimensions. H I J — Plane HIJ

Identify and name each diagram.

1. 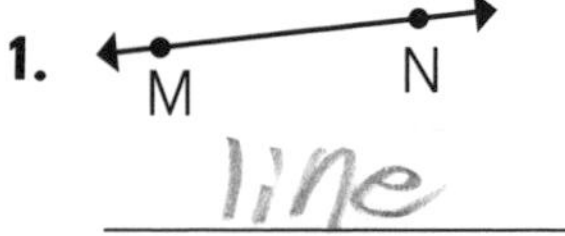

line

2. O P
segment

3. 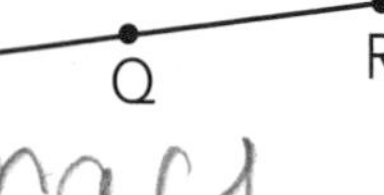

ray

4. 

plane

5. 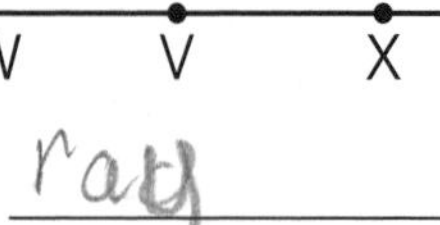

ray

6. 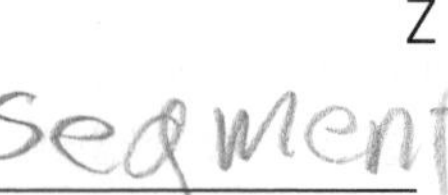

segment

Draw and label each figure.

7. Plane ABC

8. $\overrightarrow{HI}$

9. $\overleftrightarrow{XY}$

X Y

10. $\overline{ST}$

Linear Relationships

Linear Parts

Colinear points lie in a line. • A • B • C

Parallel lines never intersect.

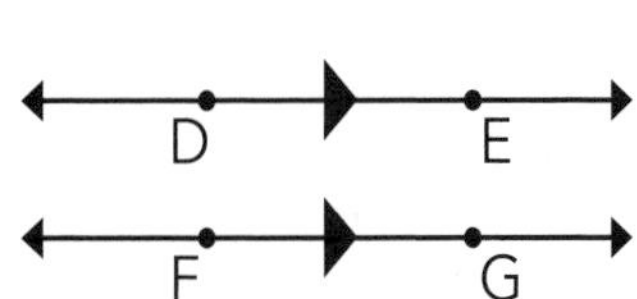

$\overleftrightarrow{DE} \parallel \overleftrightarrow{FG}$

Perpendicular lines intersect at right angles.

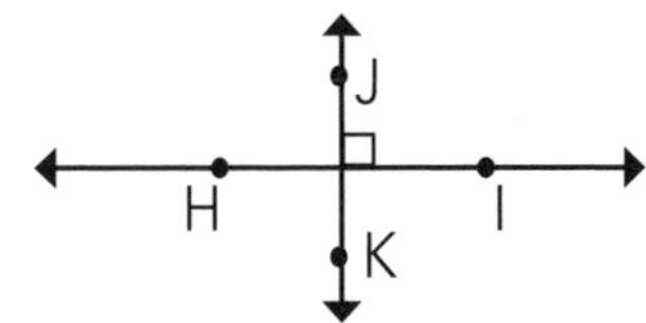

Oblique lines intersect at nonright angles.

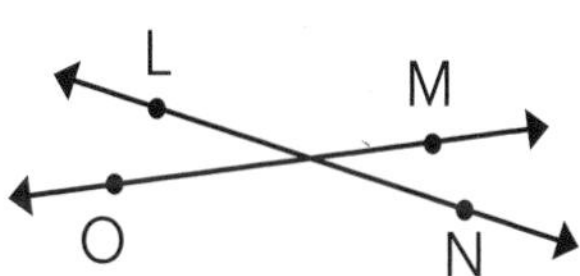

$\overleftrightarrow{LN}$ is oblique to $\overleftrightarrow{OM}$

Use the diagram to name the following items.

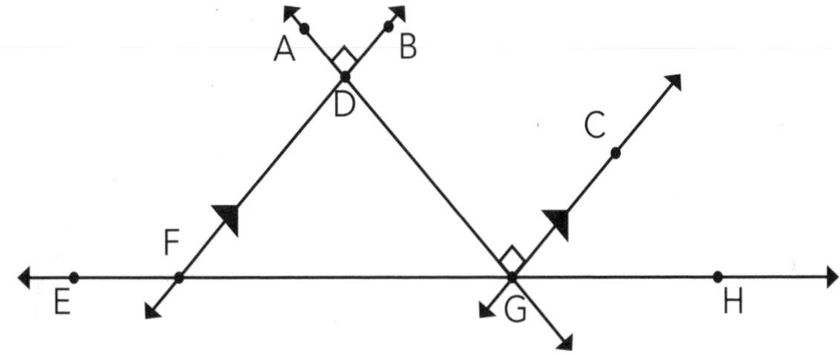

1. A pair of parallel lines
   $\overleftrightarrow{FDB} \parallel \overleftrightarrow{GC}$

2. A pair of oblique lines
   $\overleftrightarrow{ADG}$ is oblique to $\overleftrightarrow{GC}$

3. A pair of perpendicular lines
   ADG ⊥ FDB

4. Three colinear points
   ADG

5. Three noncolinear points
   DEA

6. Are two points always colinear?
   yes

Congruent Segments and Segment Addition

Linear Parts

Congruent segments have the same length.

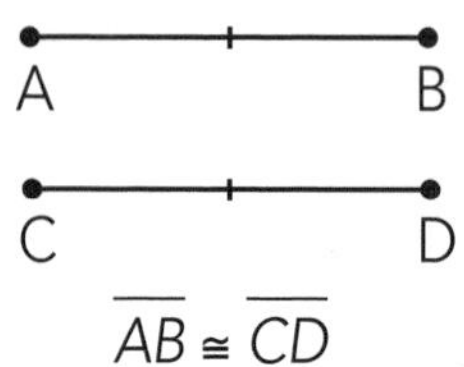

$\overline{AB} \cong \overline{CD}$

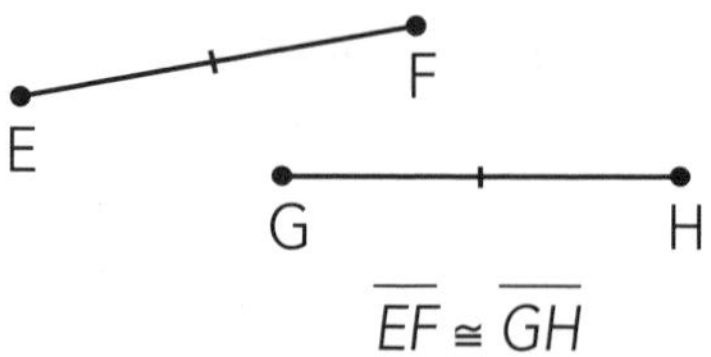

$\overline{EF} \cong \overline{GH}$

If point B lies between points A and C, then AB + BC = AC.

$AC = 10$

Find the length for each of the following segments.

A 4 B 5 C D 2 E F

1. CD = 0

2. CE = 2

3. AC = 9

4. EF = 6

5. BF = 7

6. AF = 11

Using the number line, name a segment that is congruent to each given segment.

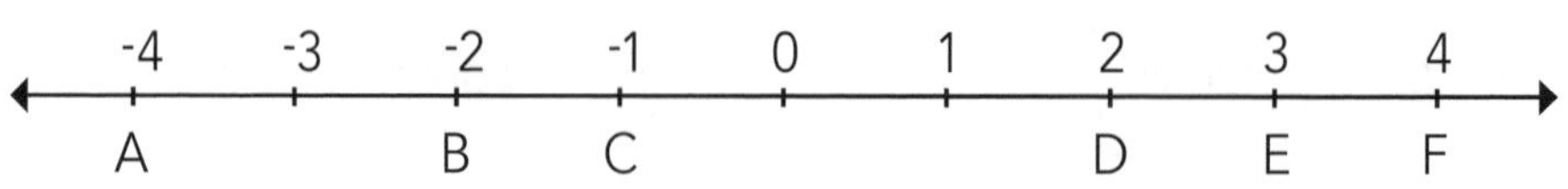

7. $\overline{AB} \cong$ DF

8. $\overline{CD} \cong$ AC

9. $\overline{EF} \cong$ BC

Midpoints

Linear Parts

A **midpoint** divides a segment into two congruent segments.

$\overline{AM} \cong \overline{MB}$

A M B

Name the point, segment, or length described.

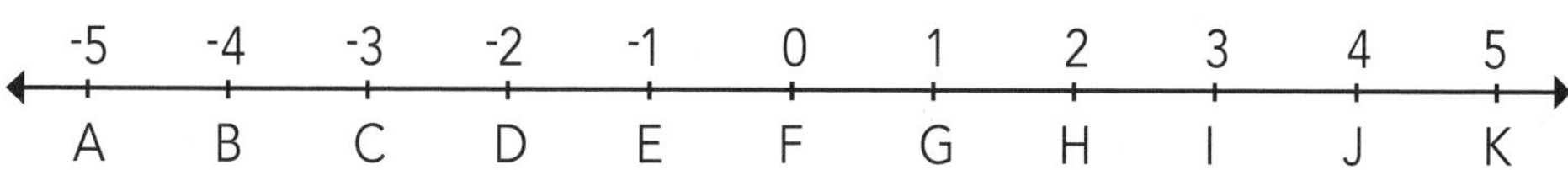

1. The midpoint of $\overline{CE}$ DE

2. The length of $\overline{FH}$ = IK

3. $\overline{HK} \cong \overline{B\_}$ E

4. The length of $\overline{CH}$ = AF

5. The midpoint of $\overline{BH}$ E

6. J is the midpoint of I K

7. The length of AK = KA

8. The midpoint of AK F

9. $\overline{GJ} \cong \overline{G\_}$ J

M is the midpoint of $\overline{AB}$ in the diagram below. Find these values.

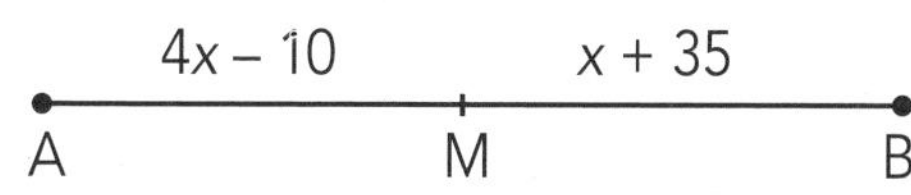

10. x = AM

11. AM = MB

12. AB = BA

Naming, Measuring, and Classifying Angles

An **angle** is formed by two rays with the same endpoint. An angle is named using three points. The **vertex** must be the middle point.

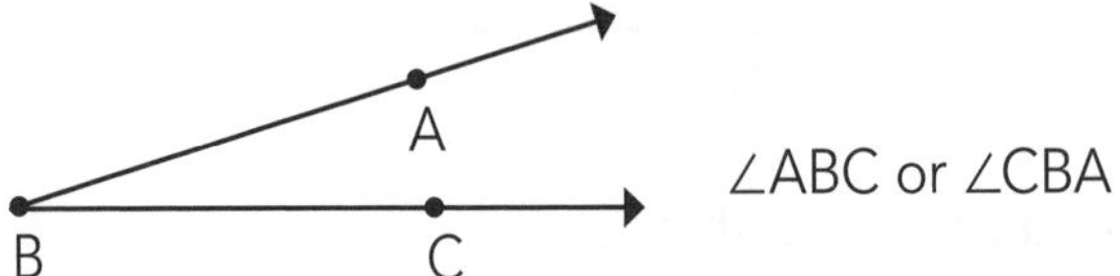

Acute angles measure between 0° and 90°, **right angles** measure exactly 90°, and **obtuse angles** measure between 90° and 180°.

Use a protractor to find the degree measure of each angle. Then, classify the angle as **acute**, **right**, or **obtuse**.

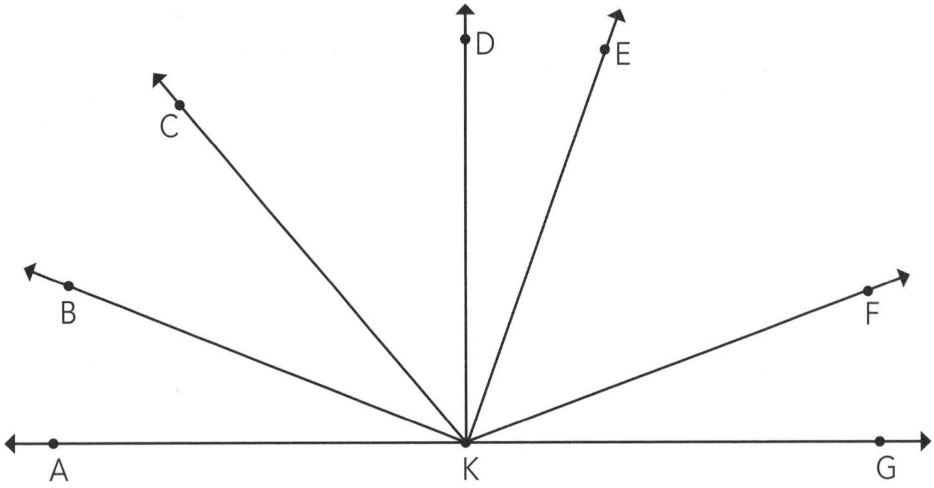

D E C B F A K G

1. ∠AKB ________ °

____

2. ∠AKD ________ °

____

3. ∠AKF ________ °

____

4. ∠CKF ________ °

____

5. ∠EKG ________ °

____

6. ∠BKG ________ °

____

7. ∠CKE ________ °

____

8. ∠DKG ________ °

____

9. ∠BKF ________ °

____

Congruent Angles and Angle Addition

Angles

Congruent angles have the same measure.

∠ABC ≅ ∠DEF

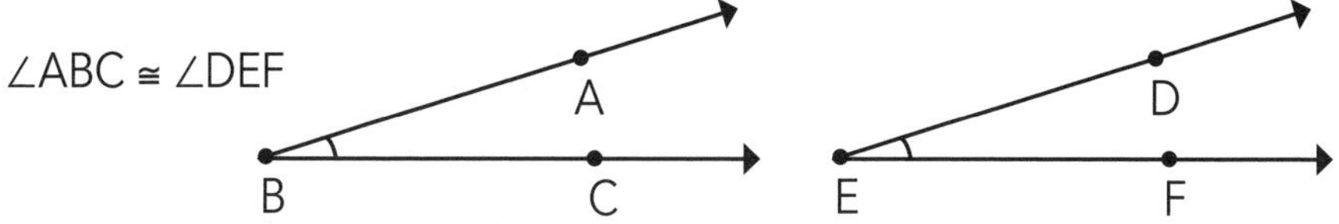

If point *W* lies in the interior of ∠XYZ, then *m*∠XYW + *m*∠WYZ = *m*∠XYZ.

m∠XYZ = 64°

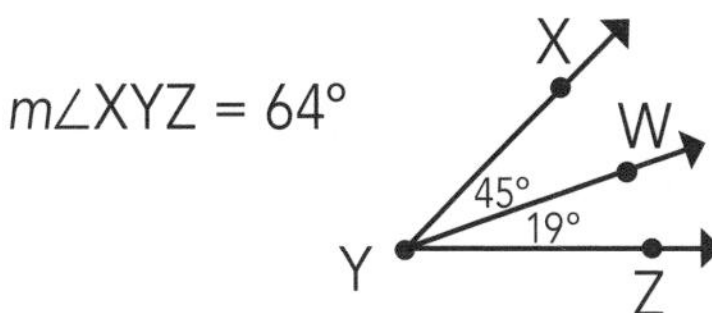

Find the missing angle measure or angle name.

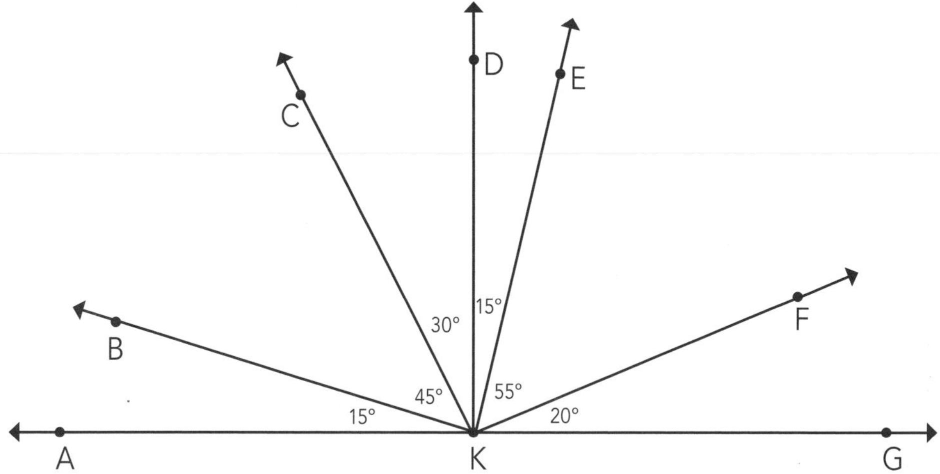

1. m∠AKC = ________°

2. m∠DKF = ________°

3. m∠BKF = ________°

4. m∠AKG = ________°

5. ∠AKD ≅ ________

6. ∠BKC ≅ ________

7. ∠EKG ≅ ________

8. m∠CKF = ________°

9. m∠AKE = ________°

10. m∠BKE = ________°

Angle Bisectors

$\overrightarrow{AB}$ bisects ∠CAD, so ∠CAB ≅ ∠BAD.

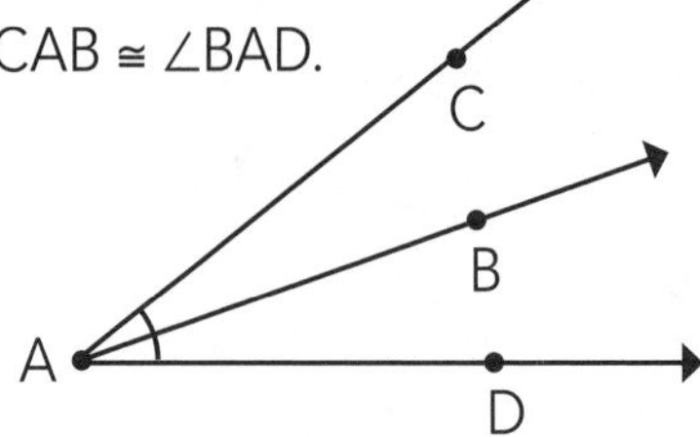

Find the missing angle measure or angle name.

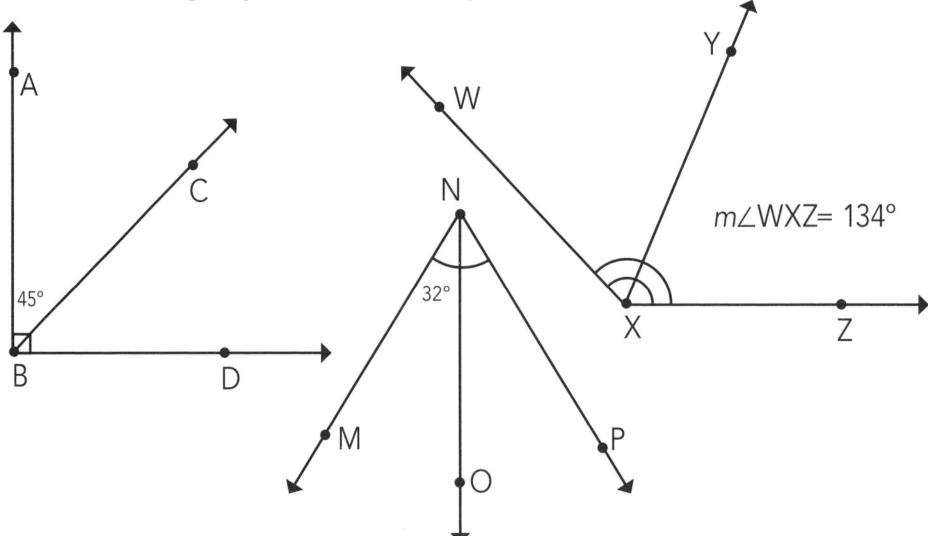

1. m∠CBD = ________________°

2. ∠ABC ≅ ________________

3. ∠ONP ≅ ________________

4. m∠ONP = ________________°

5. m∠MNP = ________________°

6. ∠WXY ≅ ________________

7. m∠WXY = ________________°

8. m∠YXZ = ________________°

9. Name the angle bisector of ∠MNP. ________________

10. Name the angle bisector of ∠WXZ. ________________

Complementary and Supplementary Angles

Angles

Complementary angles are two angles that equal 90°.

Supplementary angles are two angles that equal 180°.

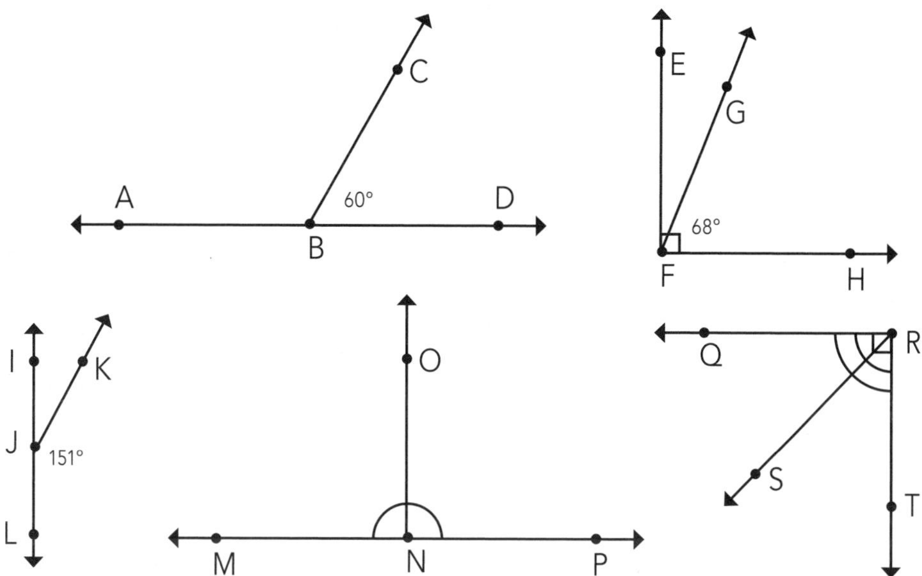

Find the missing angle measure or angle name.

1. An angle supplementary to ∠CBD = ____________________
2. m∠ABC = ____________ °
3. m∠EFG = ____________ °
4. An angle complementary to m∠EFG = ____________________
5. m∠IJK = ____________ °
6. ∠MNO ≅ ____________
7. m∠SRT = ____________ °
8. Find the complement of a 27° angle. ____________________
9. Find the supplement of a 45° angle. ____________________
10. Find the supplement of the complement of a 70° angle. __________

Vertical Angles

Vertical angles are created by intersecting lines.
Vertical angles are congruent.

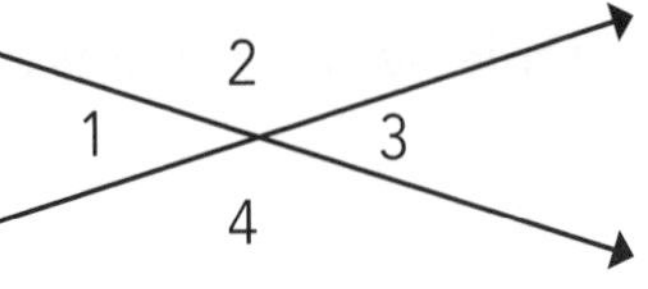

Angle 1 and ∠3 are vertical angles, so ∠1 ≅ ∠3.

Angle 2 and ∠4 are vertical angles, so ∠2 ≅ ∠4.

Find the missing angle measure or angle name.

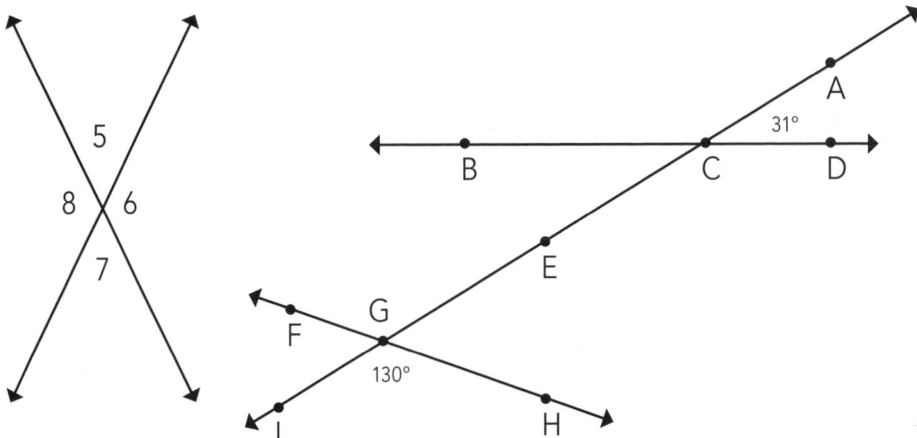

1. ∠5 ≅ ____________________

2. ∠6 is vertical to ____________

3. m∠BCE = ________________ °

4. m∠BCA = ________________ °

5. m∠DCE= ________________ °

6. m∠FGE = ________________ °

7. m∠FGI = ________________ °

8. m∠EGH = ________________ °

9. The four angles created by the intersection of two lines will always equal ______ degrees.

Corresponding Angles

Angles

Corresponding angles are formed when a line (**transversal**) intersects two or more parallel lines. In the diagram below, line *t* intersects lines *m* and *n*. The intersections create eight angles.

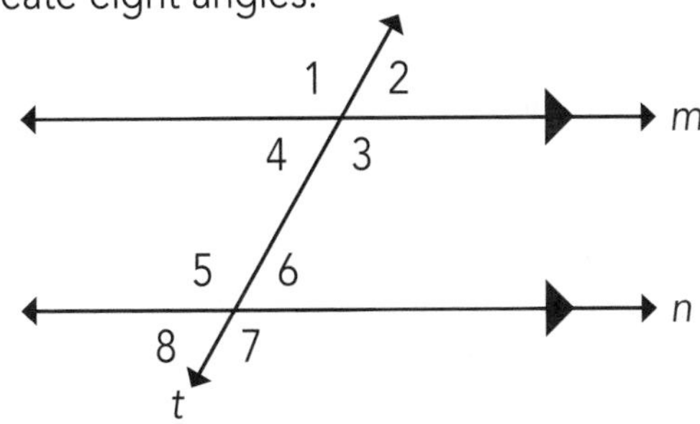

Corresponding angles are angles that sit in the same position at each intersection. For example, ∠1 and ∠5 are corresponding angles because both angles sit in the upper left corner of each intersection.

Other corresponding angle pairs include: ∠2 and ∠6, ∠3 and ∠7, ∠4 and ∠8.

Corresponding Angles Postulate: If two parallel lines are intersected by a transversal, then the corresponding angles that are formed are congruent.

In the above diagram, ∠1 ≅ ∠5, ∠2 ≅ ∠6, ∠3 ≅ ∠7, ∠4 ≅ ∠8.

Solve for x in each diagram.

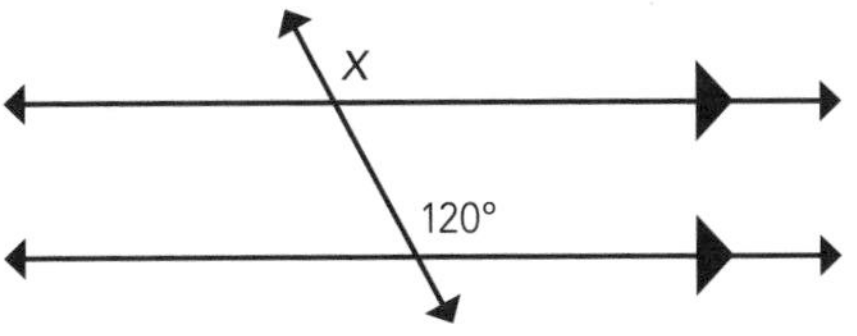

1. x = ____________________

117°

x

2. x = ____________________

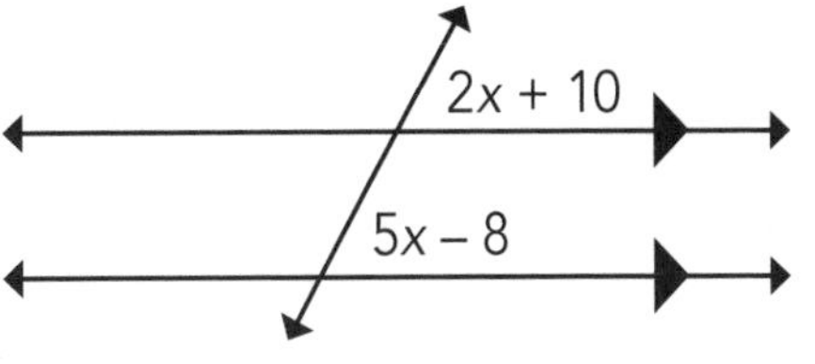

3. x = ____________________

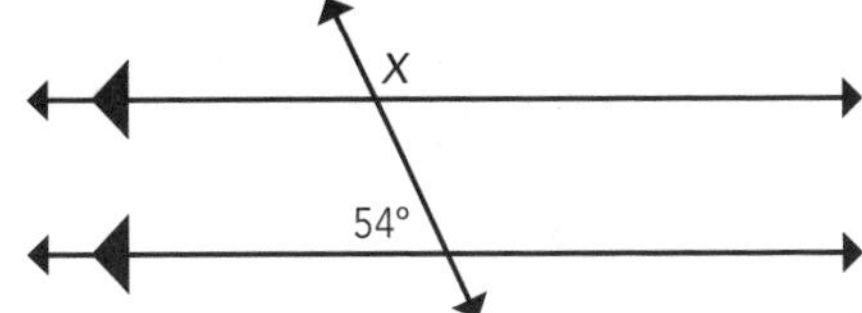

4. x = ____________________

Alternate Interior and Exterior Angles

Alternate interior and **alternate exterior angles** are formed when a line (**transversal**) intersects two or more parallel lines. In the diagram, line *t* intersects lines *m* and *n*. The intersections create eight angles.

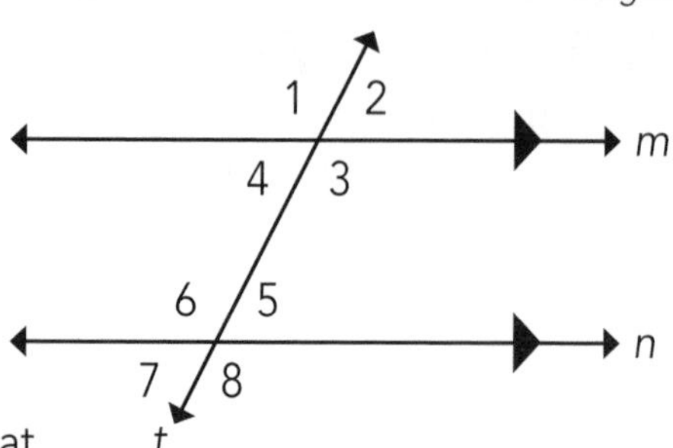

Alternate interior angles are angles that sit inside the parallel lines and on alternate sides of the transversal. For example, ∠3 and ∠6 are alternate interior angles.

Alternate exterior angles are angles that sit outside the parallel lines and on alternate sides of the transversal. For example, ∠1 and ∠8 are alternate exterior angles.

Alternate Interior Angles Theorem: If two parallel lines are intersected by a transversal, then the alternate interior angles are congruent.

Alternate Exterior Angles Theorem: If two parallel lines are intersected by a transversal, then the alternate exterior angles are congruent.

In the above diagram, the following angles are congruent: $\angle 1 \cong \angle 8$, $\angle 2 \cong \angle 7$, $\angle 3 \cong \angle 6$, $\angle 4 \cong \angle 5$.

Solve for x in each diagram.

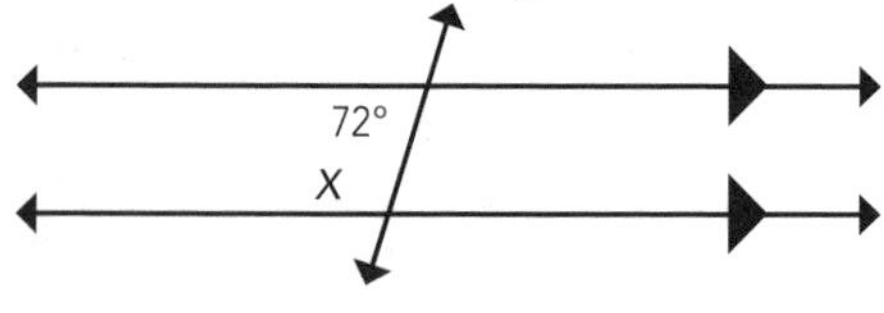

1. x = ______________________

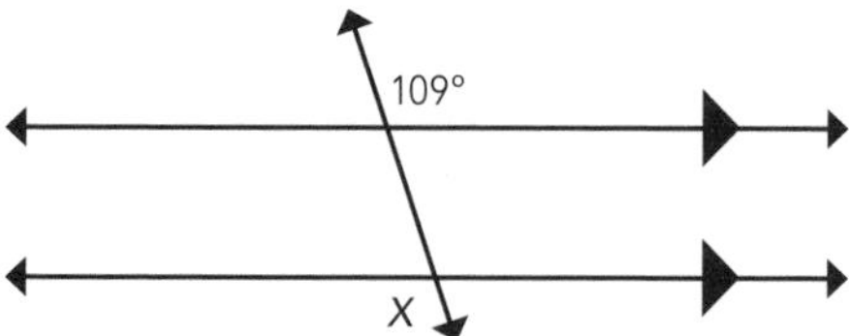

2. x = ______________________

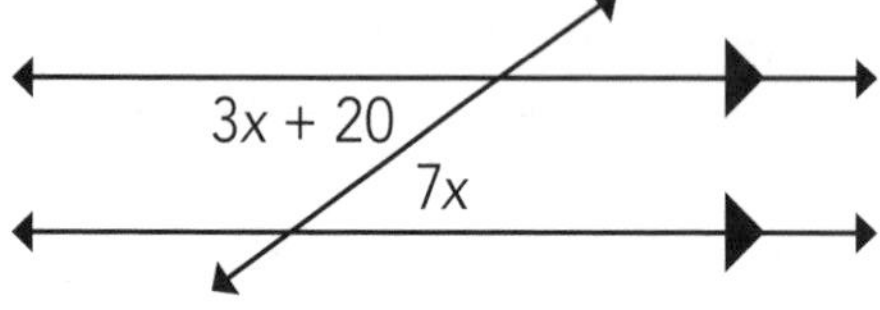

3. x = ______________________

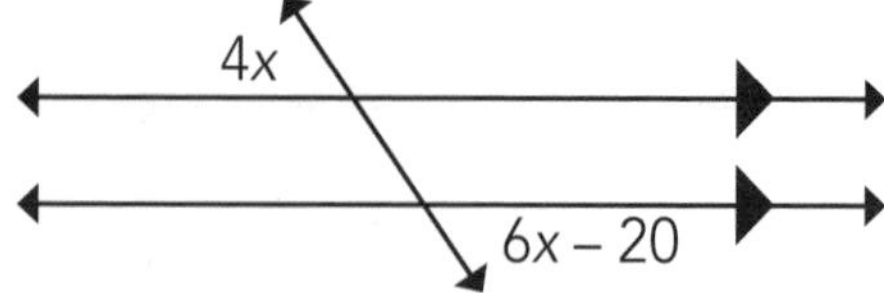

4. x = ______________________

Same-Side Interior Angles

Angles

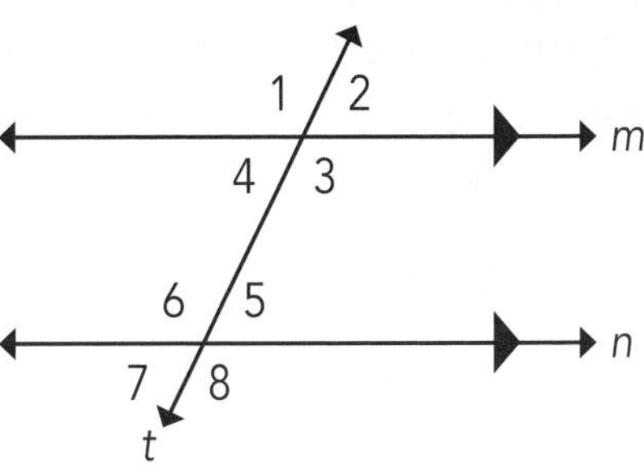

Same-side interior angles are formed when a line (**transversal**) intersects two or more parallel lines. In the diagram, line *t* intersects lines *m* and *n*. The intersections create eight angles.

Same-side interior angles are angles that sit inside the parallel lines and on the same side of the transversal. Angle 3 and $\angle 5$ are same-side interior angles; so are $\angle 4$ and $\angle 6$.

Same-Side Interior Angles Theorem: If two parallel lines are intersected by a transversal, then the same-side interior angles that are formed are supplementary.

In the above diagram, $m\angle 3 + m\angle 5 = 180°$ and $m\angle 4 + m\angle 6 = 180°$.

Solve for x in each diagram.

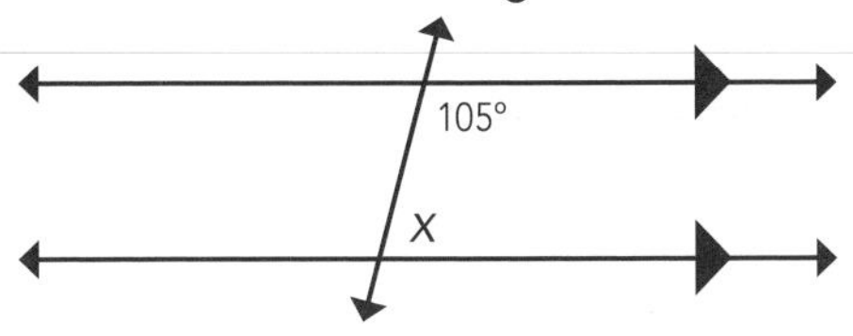

1. x = ______________________

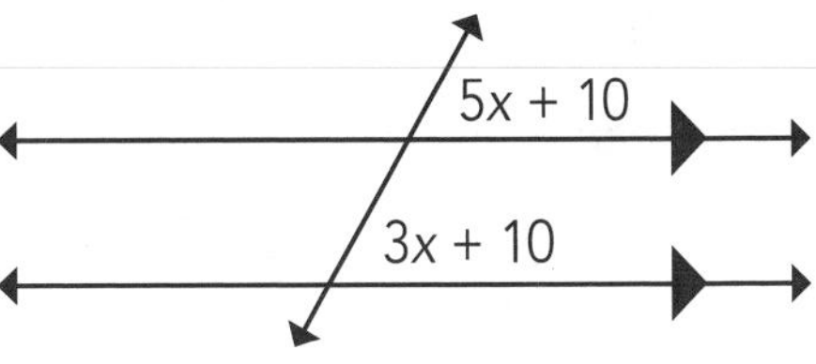

2. x = ______________________

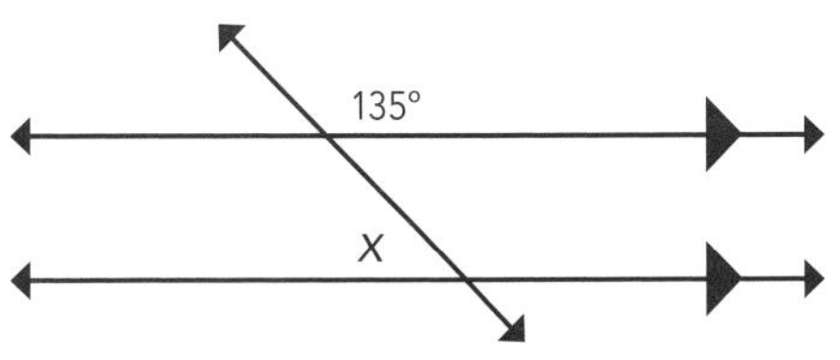

3. x = ______________________

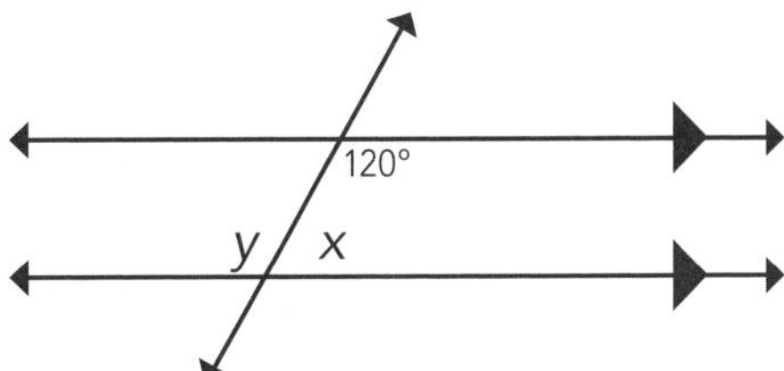

4. x = ______________________

y = ______________________

Classifying Polygons

A **polygon** is a closed figure made of segments that intersect only at endpoints.

1. Determine which figure(s) are polygons. Circle your answers.

A.

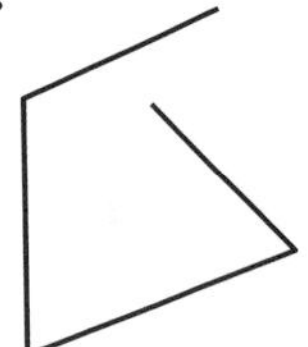

B.

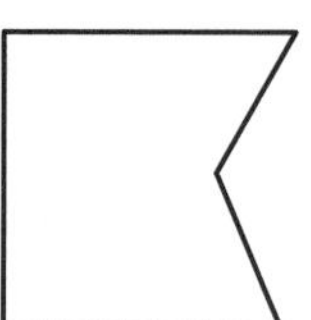

C.

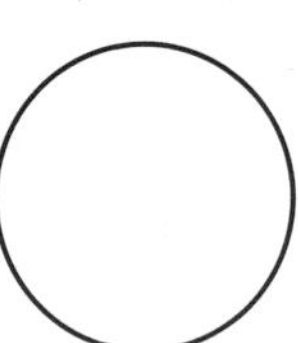

D.

Polygons are named by the number of sides they have.

3 sides—triangle

4 sides—quadrilateral

5 sides—pentagon

6 sides—hexagon

7 sides—heptagon

8 sides—octagon

Name each polygon according to the number of sides it has.

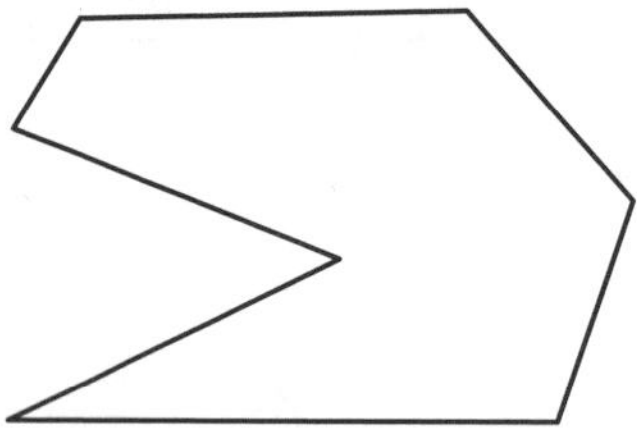

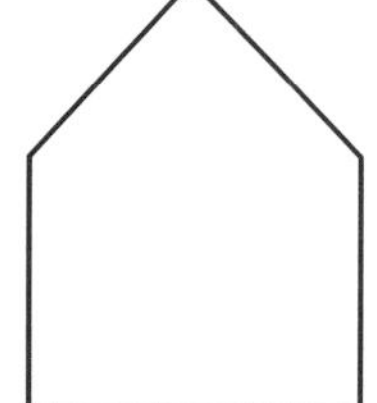

2. ______________________

3. ______________________

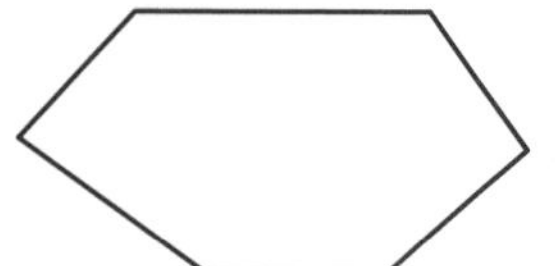

4. ______________________

5. ______________________

Polygon Angle Measures

Polygons

The sum of the measures of the interior angles of a polygon with *n* sides can be found by the formula $S = (n - 2) \bullet 180°$.

Find the sums of the measures of the interior angles for these polygons.

1. hexagon = ____________

2. quadrilateral = ____________

3. octagon = ____________

4. heptagon = ____________

5. pentagon = ____________

6. triangle = ____________

Find the measure of the angle marked x.

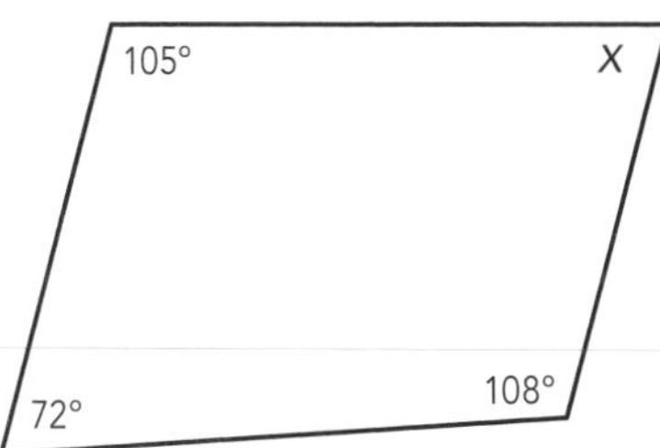

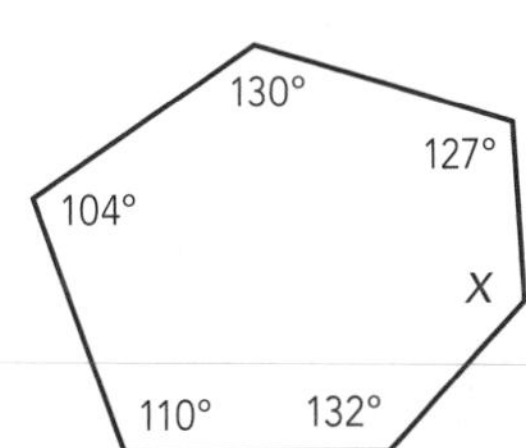

7. x = ____________

8. x = ____________

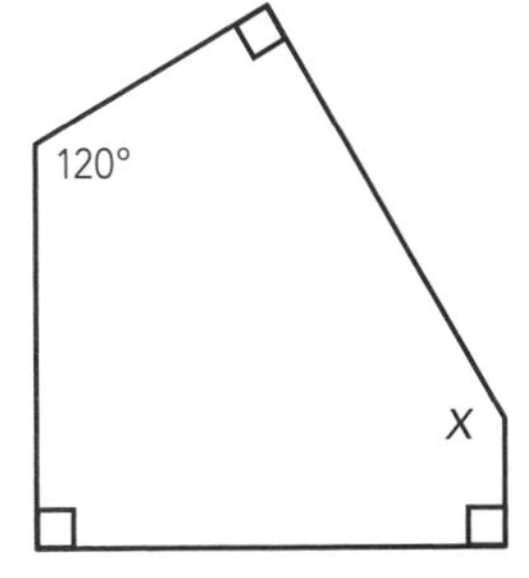

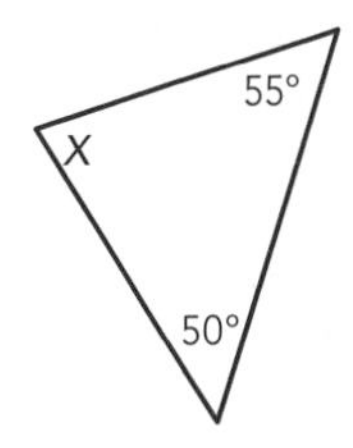

9. x = ____________

10. x = ____________

Regular and Irregular Polygons

A **regular polygon** has all sides congruent (**equilateral**) and all angles congruent (**equiangular**). **Irregular polygons** have sides of different lengths, angles of different measure, or both.

Determine if the polygon is regular or irregular.

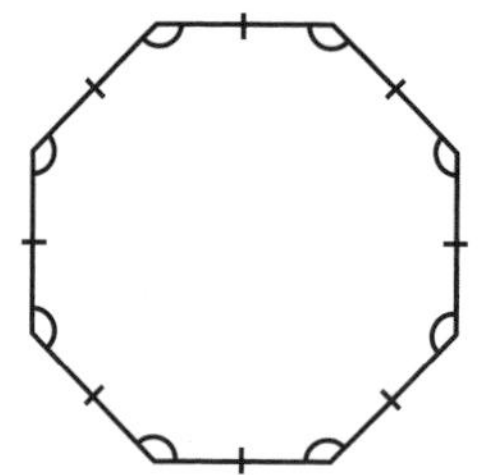

1. ______________________ **2.** ______________________

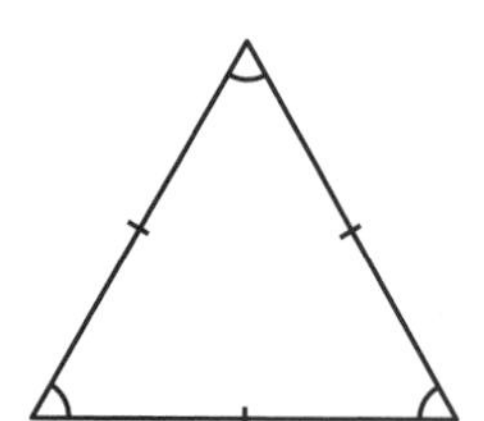

3. ______________________ **4.** ______________________

Find the measure of one interior angle for each regular polygon. Round answers to the nearest hundredth if necessary.

5. triangle = ______________ ° **6.** quadrilateral = ______________ °

7. pentagon = ______________ ° **8.** hexagon = ______________ °

9. heptagon = ______________ ° **10.** octagon = ______________ °

Drawing Polygons

Polygons

A **convex polygon** has all angles pointing outward. The following polygons are examples of convex polygons.

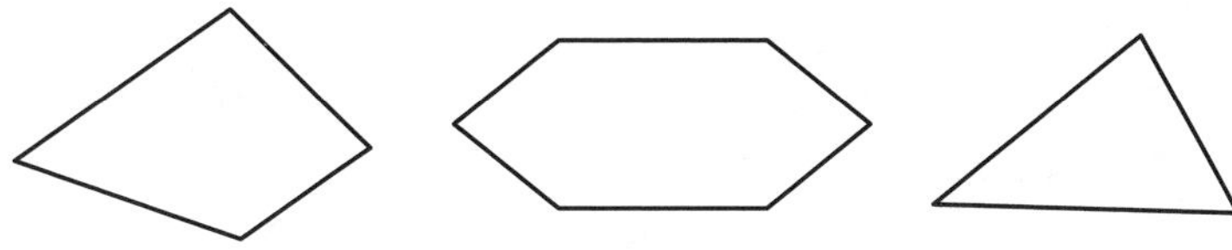

A **concave polygon** has at least one angle pointing inward. The following polygons are examples of concave polygons.

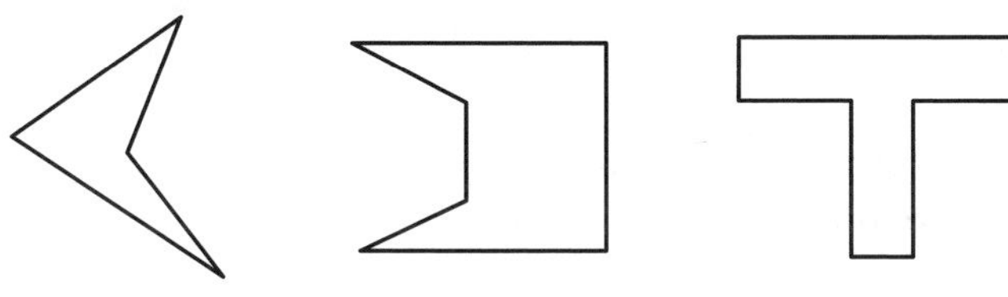

Draw each polygon.

1. an irregular pentagon

2. a regular hexagon

3. a convex quadrilateral

4. a concave quadrilateral

5. a regular octagon

6. an irregular octagon

Congruent Polygons

Two polygons are congruent if their corresponding side lengths and angle measures are congruent.

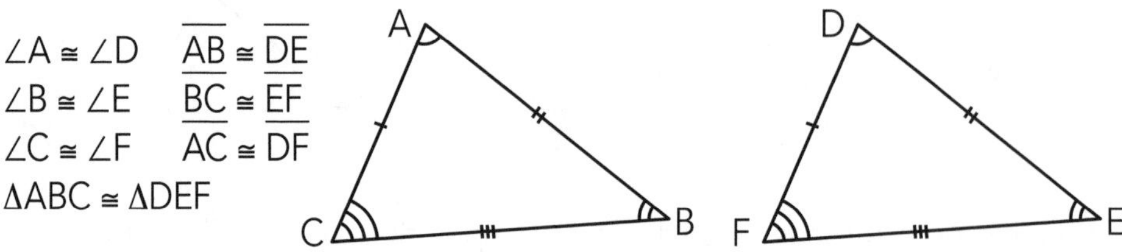

Find the missing angle measures or angle names.

pentagon ABCDE ≅ pentagon VWXYZ

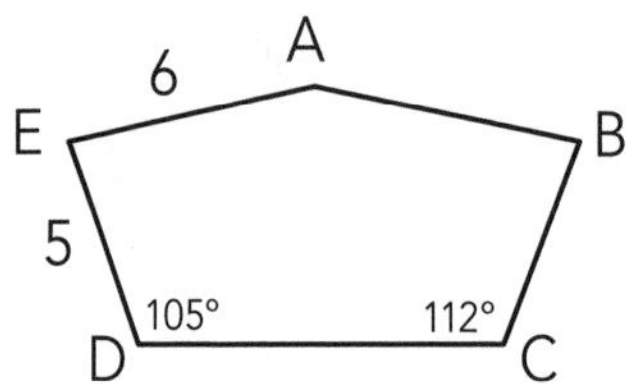

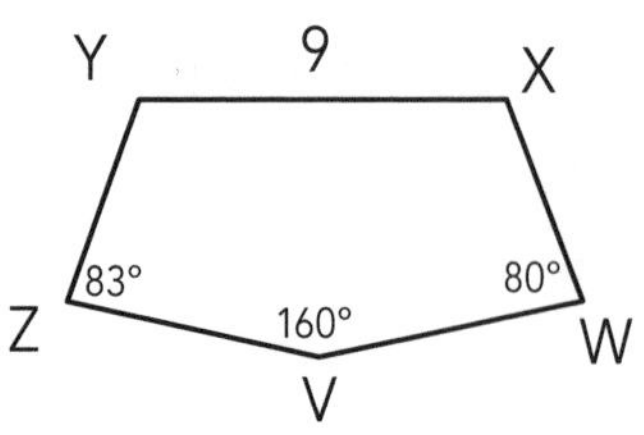

1. $\angle A \cong$ ____________________ **2.** $\overline{DC} \cong$ ____________________

3. $m\angle Y =$ ____________________° **4.** $\overline{AB} \cong$ ____________________

5. $\overline{VZ} =$ ____________________ **6.** $m\angle E =$ ____________________°

7. $m\angle B =$ ____________________° **8.** $\overline{YZ} =$ ____________________

Classifying Triangles

Triangles

Classifying by angle measures: An **acute triangle** has three acute angles.
A **right triangle** has one right angle.
An **obtuse triangle** has one obtuse angle.

Classifying by side lengths: A **scalene triangle** has no congruent sides.
An **isosceles triangle** has at least two congruent sides.
An **equilateral triangle** has three congruent sides.

Classify each triangle both by angle measures and side lengths.

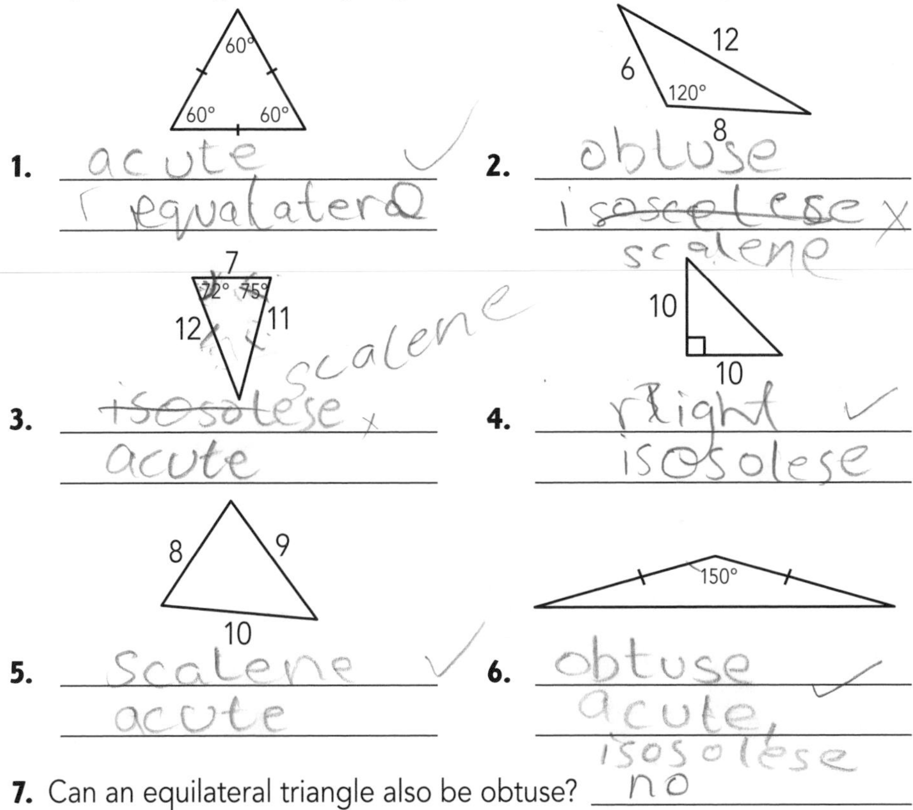

7. Can an equilateral triangle also be obtuse? __________

8. Can an equilateral triangle also be right? __________

9. Can an equilateral triangle also be acute? __________

Triangle Sum Theorem

The **interior angles** of a triangle equal 180°.

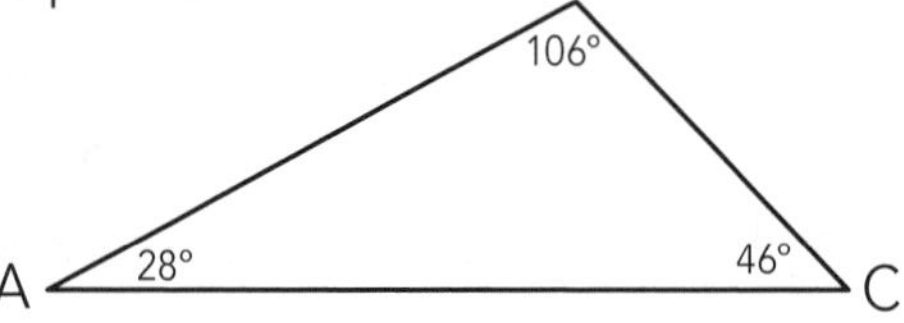

$m\angle A + m\angle B + m\angle C = 180°$

Find the missing angle measure for each triangle.

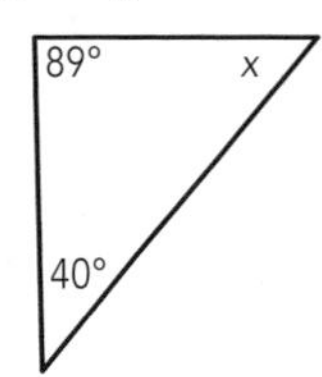

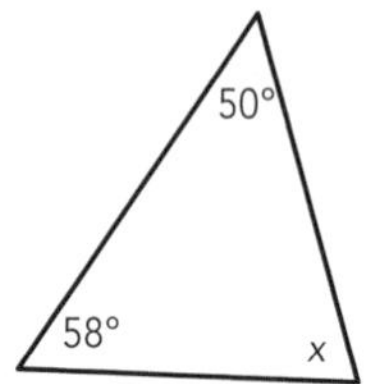

1. x = ____________________

2. x = ____________________

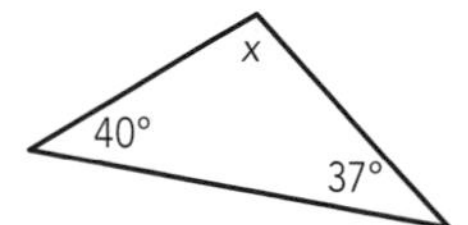

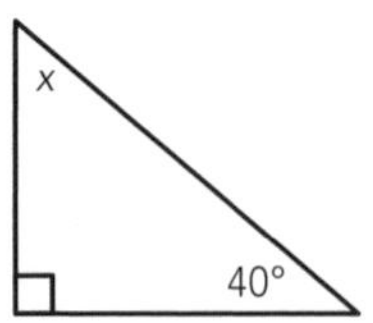

3. x = ____________________

4. x = ____________________

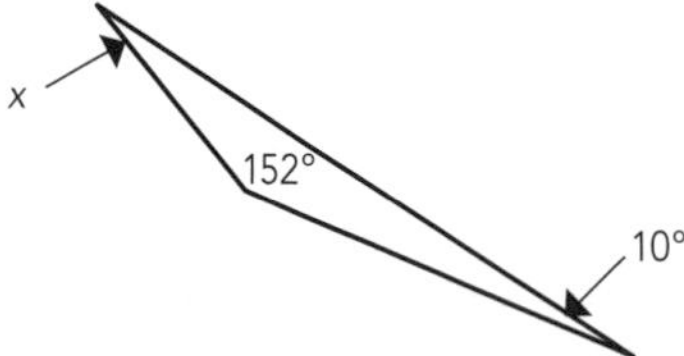

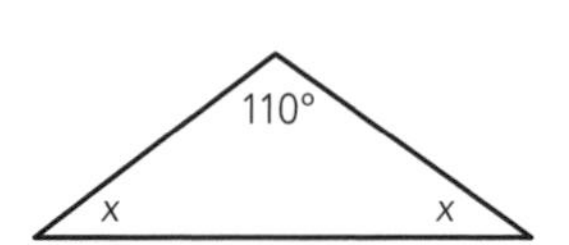

5. x = ____________________

6. x = ____________________

Angle Measures of Triangles

Triangles

The two base angles of an isosceles triangle are congruent. All three angles of an equilateral triangle are congruent.

Find the missing measures in each triangle.

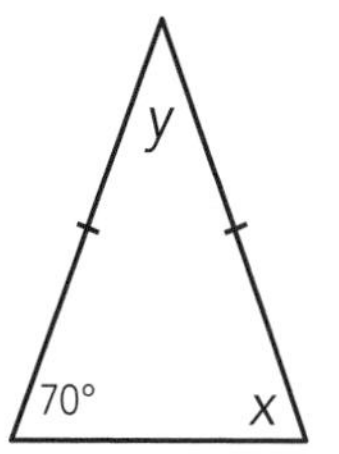

1. x = _____° y = _____°

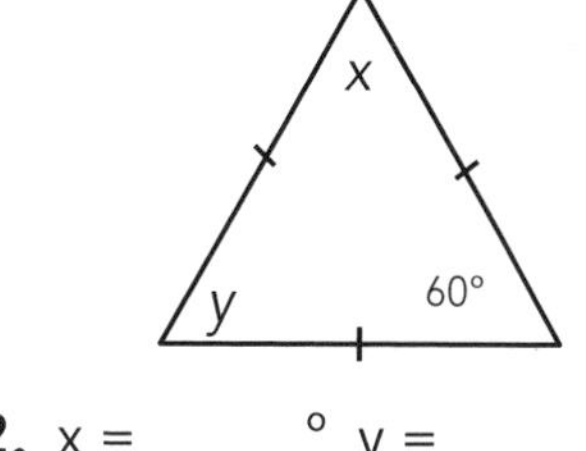

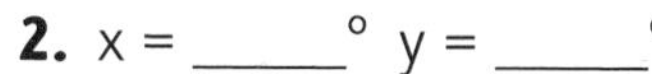

2. x = _____° y = _____°

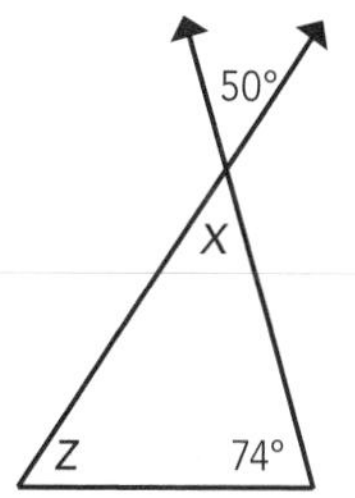

3. x = _____° z = _____°

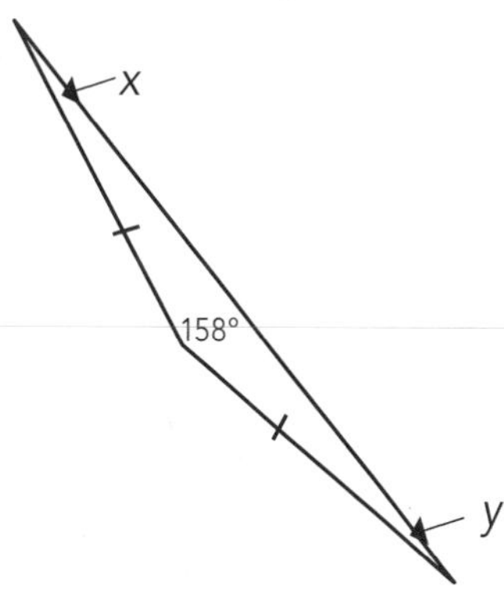

4. x = _____° y = _____°

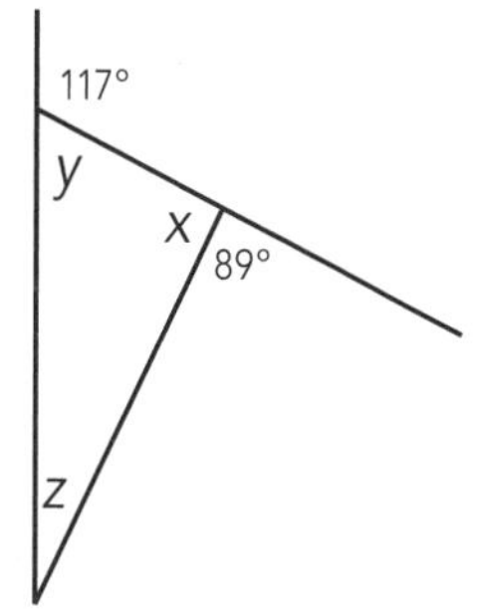

5. x = _____° y = _____° z = _____°

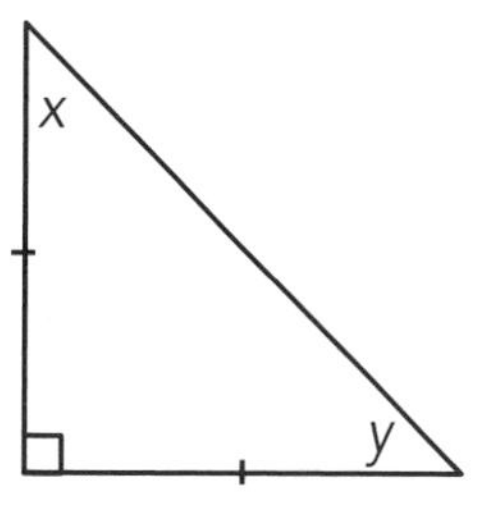

6. x = _____° y = _____°

Angle Puzzle

Triangles

Using the given information, fill in the measures of the rest of the angles in this picture.

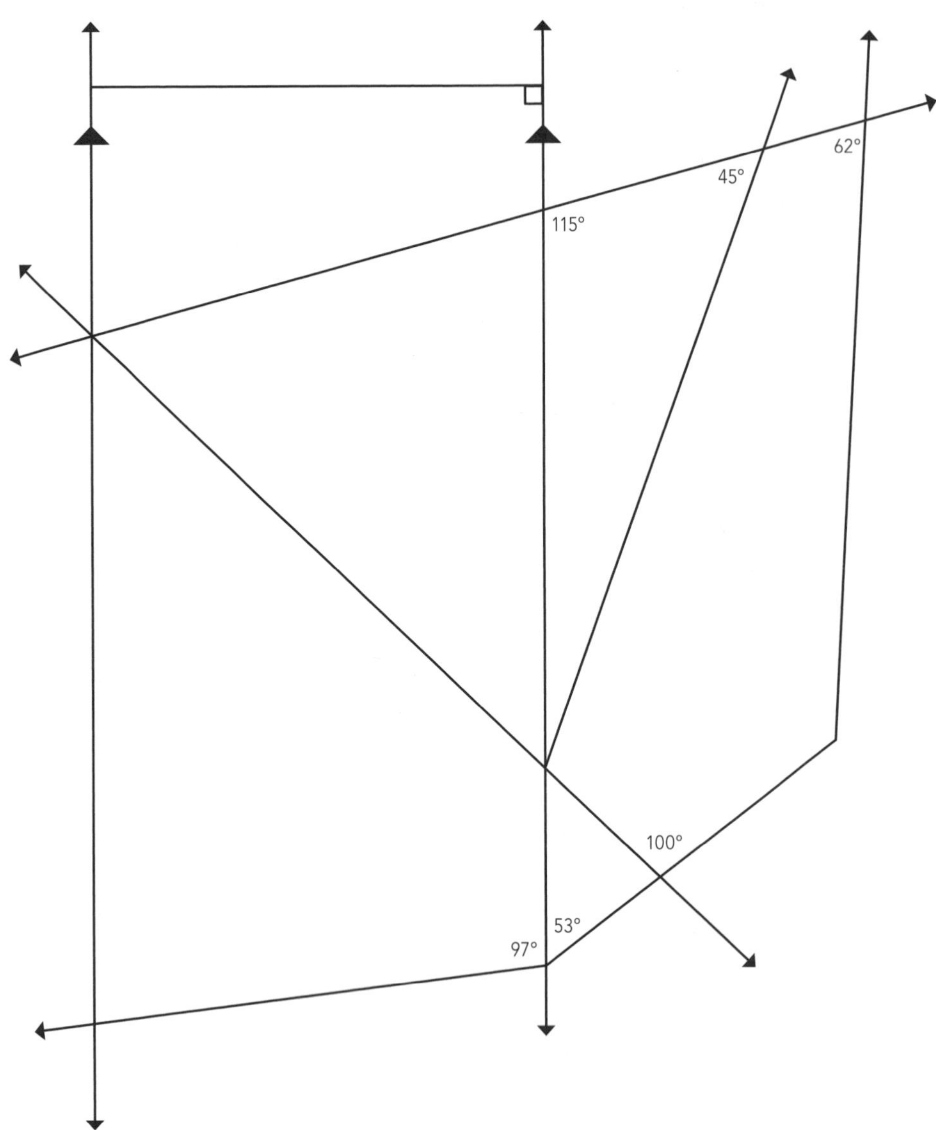

Congruent Triangles

Triangles

Two triangles are congruent if:

- All three pairs of corresponding sides are congruent. (**SSS**)

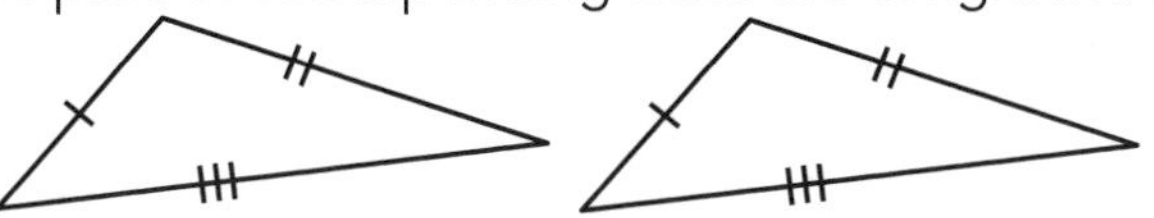

- Two corresponding sides and the included angles are congruent. (**SAS**)

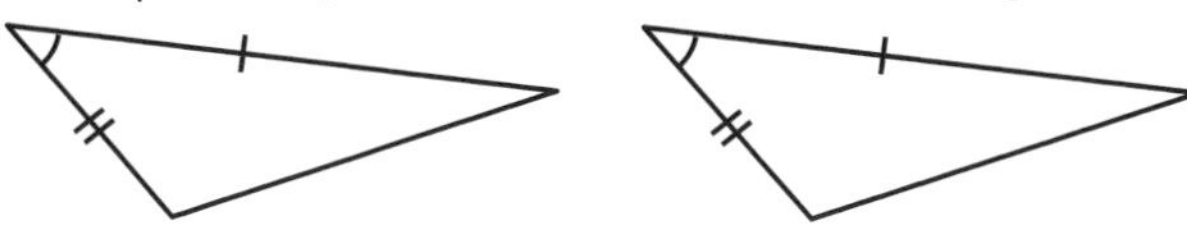

Determine if each pair of triangles is congruent. If so, state the property that makes them congruent.

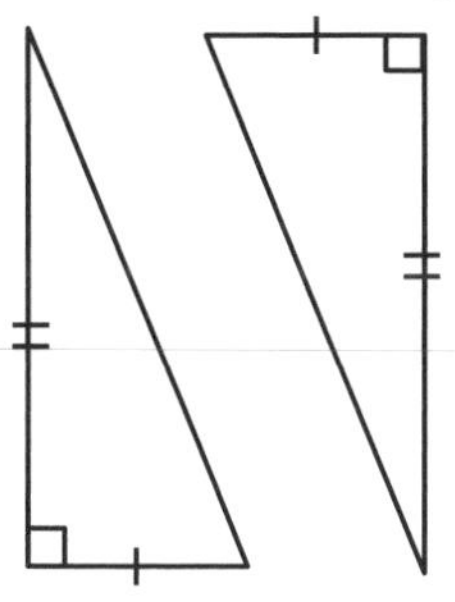

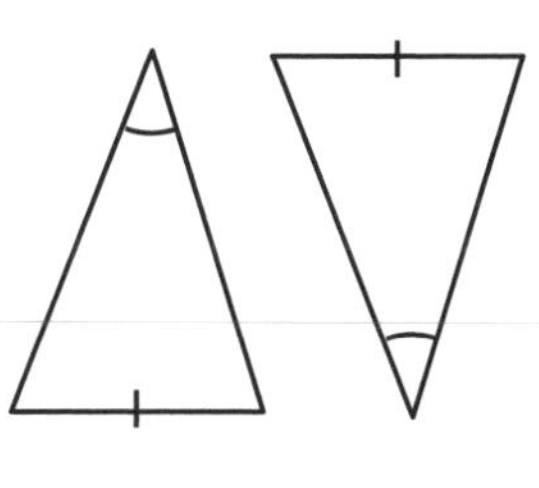

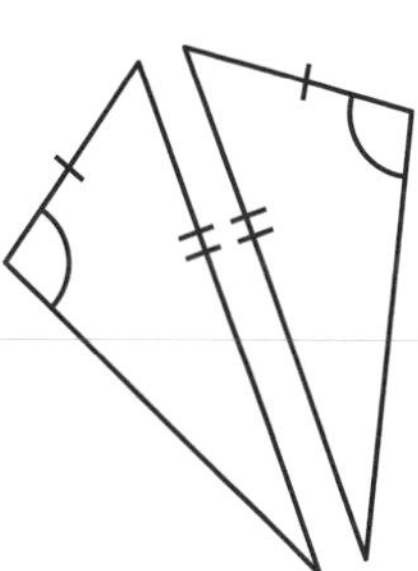

1. ______________ **2.** ______________ **3.** ______________

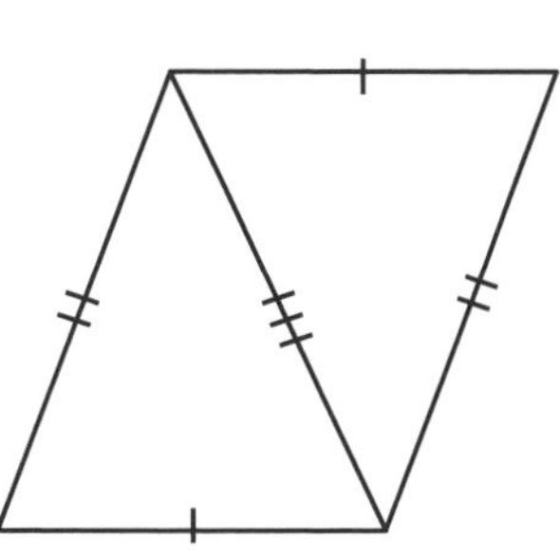

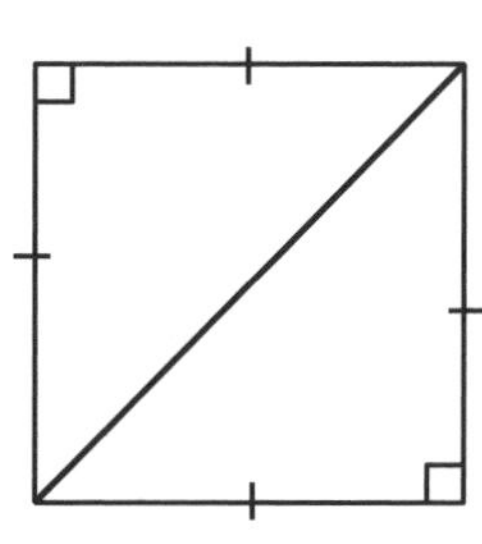

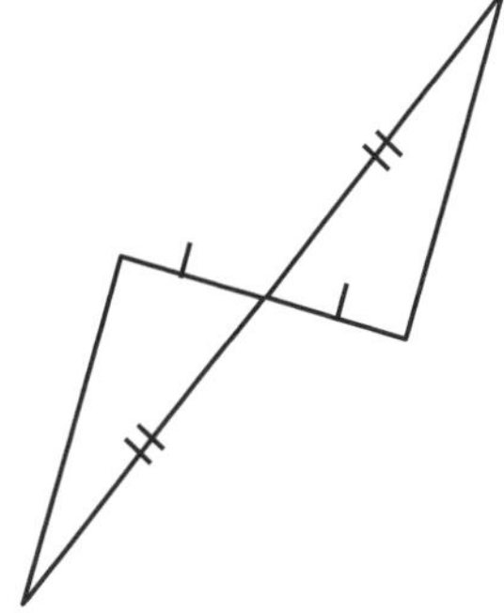

4. ______________ **5.** ______________ **6.** ______________

Congruent Triangles, continued

Two triangles are congruent if:

- Two corresponding angles and the included side are congruent. (**ASA**)

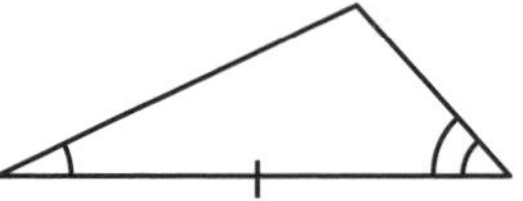
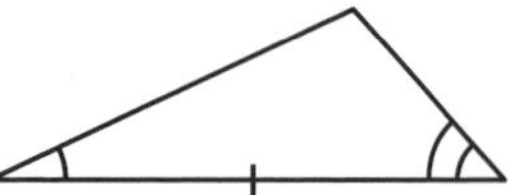

- Two corresponding angles and a nonincluded side are congruent. (**AAS**)

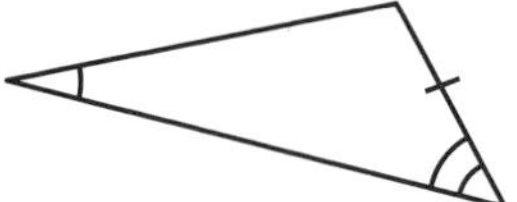
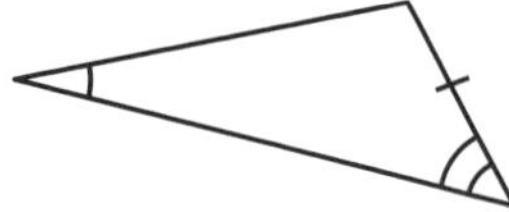

- They are right triangles in which the hypotenuse and one leg of each triangle are congruent. (**HL**)

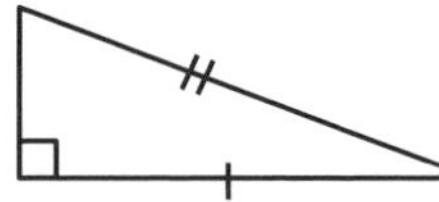
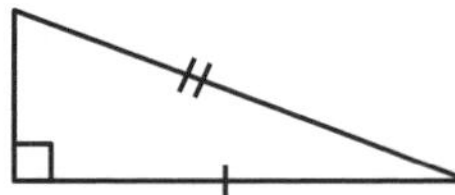

Determine if each pair of triangles is congruent. If so, state the property that makes them congruent.

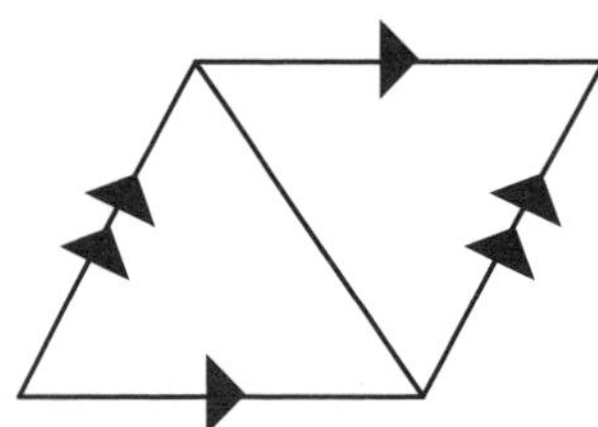
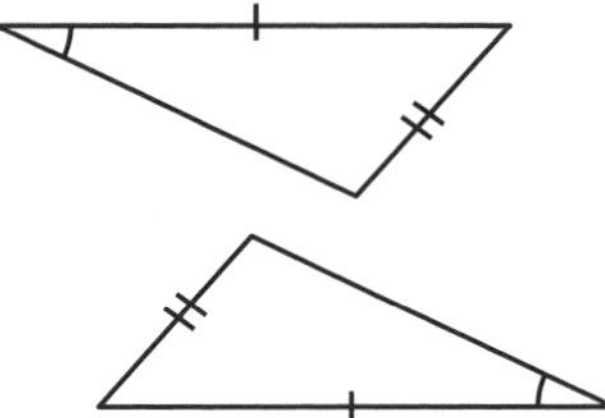
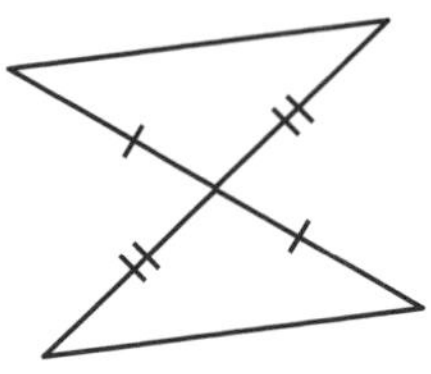

1. ______________ **2.** ______________ **3.** ______________

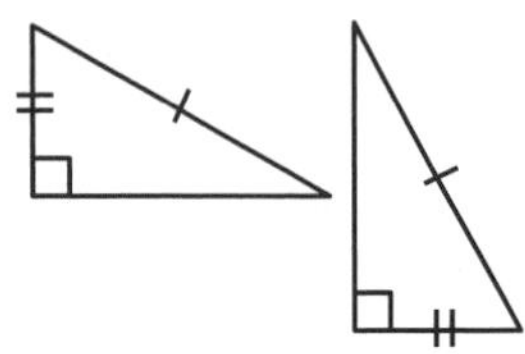
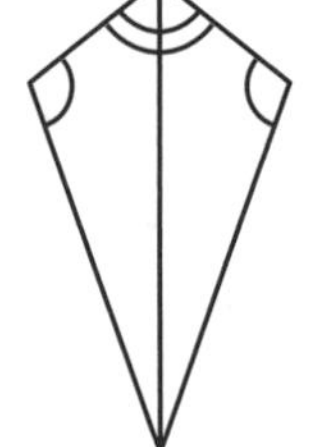
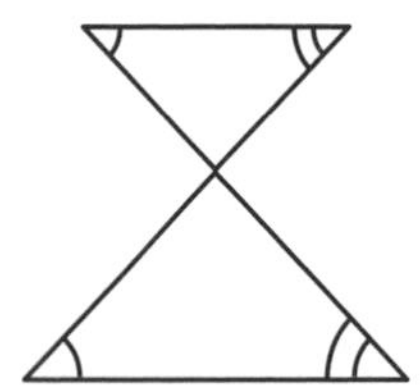

4. ______________ **5.** ______________ **6.** ______________

Parts of Congruent Triangles

Triangles

Corresponding parts of congruent triangles are congruent.

$\angle A \cong \angle D$ $\quad \overline{AB} \cong \overline{DE}$

$\angle B \cong \angle E$ $\quad \overline{BC} \cong \overline{EF}$

$\angle C \cong \angle F$ $\quad \overline{AC} \cong \overline{DF}$

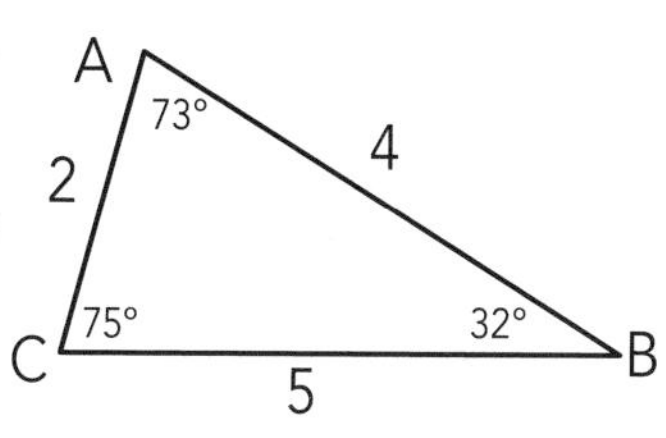

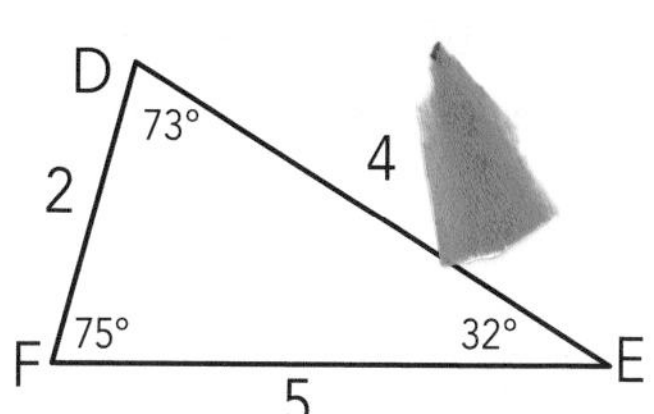

Find the missing measures for each pair of congruent triangles.

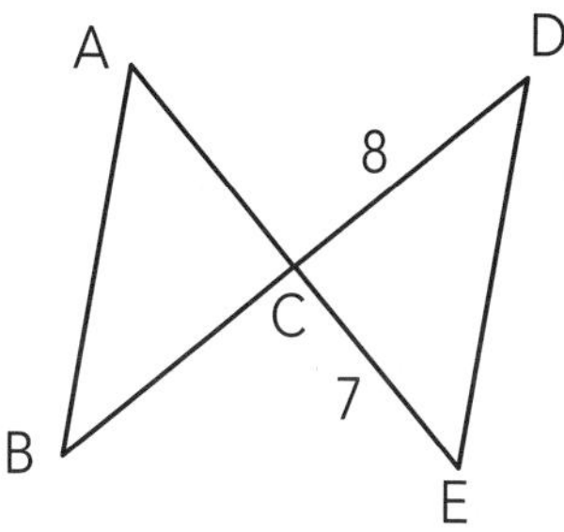

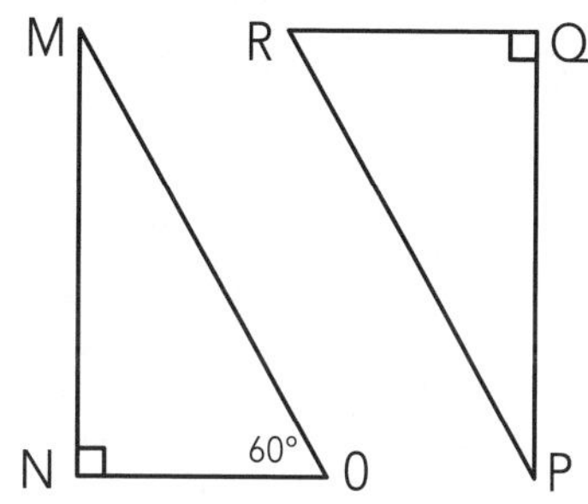

1. $\Delta ABC \cong \Delta DEC$ $\quad \overline{AC}$ = ______

2. $\Delta MNO \cong \Delta PQR$ $\quad m\angle P$ = ______°

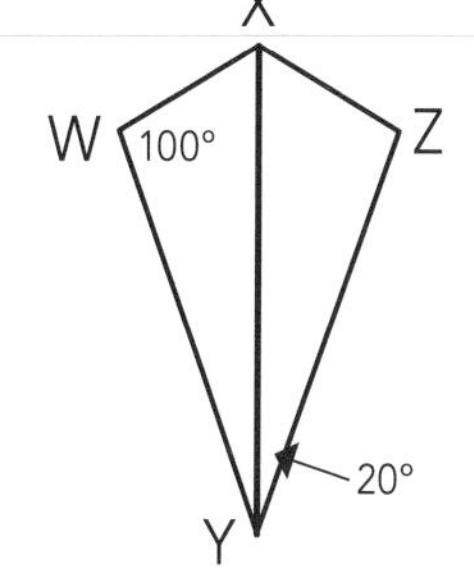

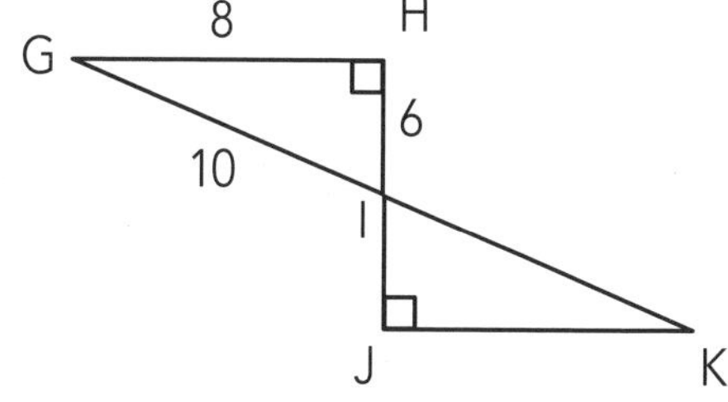

3. $\Delta XYW \cong \Delta XYZ$ $\quad m\angle YXZ$ = ______°

4. $\Delta GHI \cong \Delta KJI$ $\quad \overline{IK}$ = ______

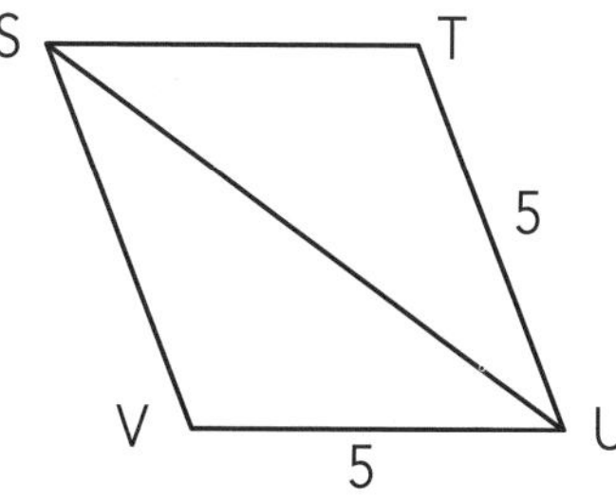

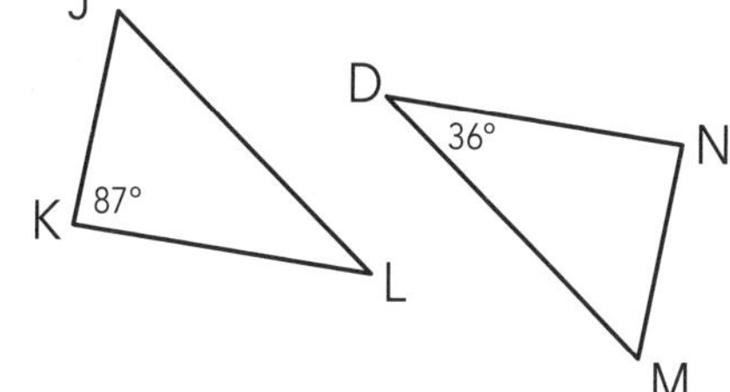

5. $\Delta STU \cong \Delta UVS$ $\quad \overline{ST}$ = ______

6. $\Delta JKL \cong \Delta MND$ $\quad m\angle J$ = ______°

The Pythagorean Theorem

For a right triangle, the sum of the squares of the legs of the triangle equals the square of the hypotenuse. The **hypotenuse** is the side opposite the right angle.

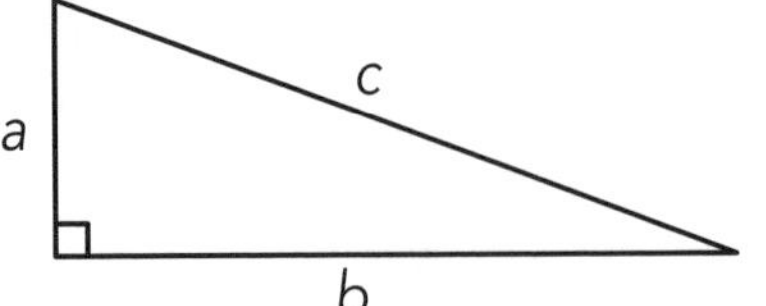

$a^2 + b^2 = c^2$

In the triangle above, sides *a* and *b* are the legs of the triangle, while side *c* is the hypotenuse.

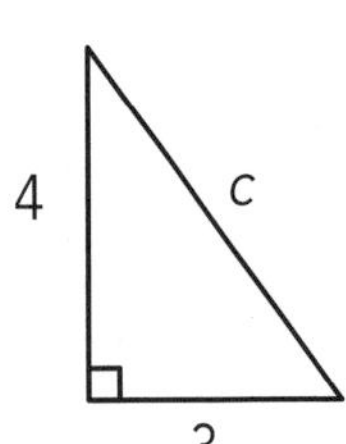

$a^2 + b^2 = c^2$
$3^2 + 4^2 = c^2$
$9 + 16 = c^2$
$25 = c^2$
$c = \sqrt{25}$
$c = 5$

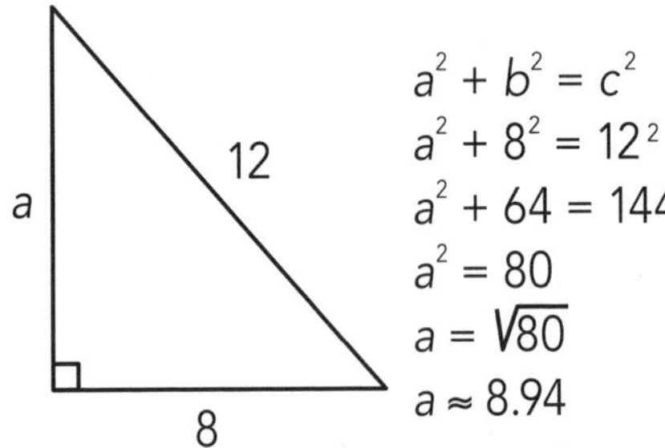

$a^2 + b^2 = c^2$
$a^2 + 8^2 = 12^2$
$a^2 + 64 = 144$
$a^2 = 80$
$a = \sqrt{80}$
$a \approx 8.94$

Find the missing side lengths. Round your answers to the nearest hundredth.

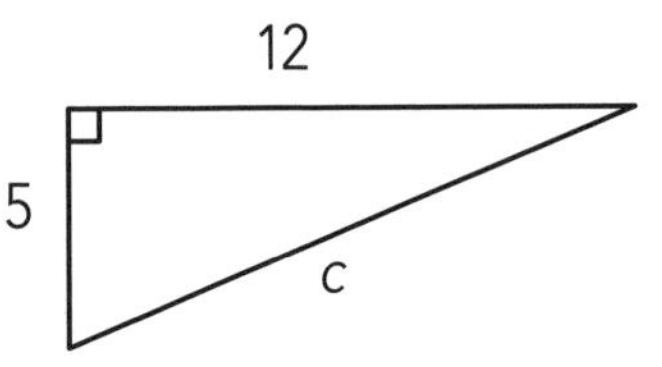

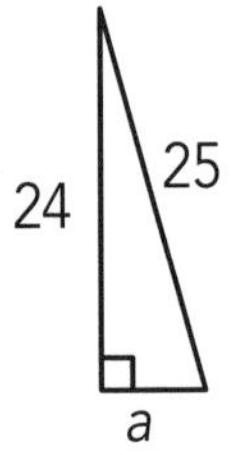

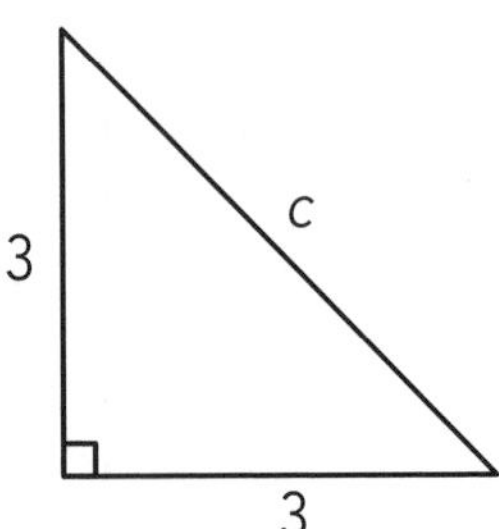

1. c = __________ **2.** a = __________ **3.** c = __________

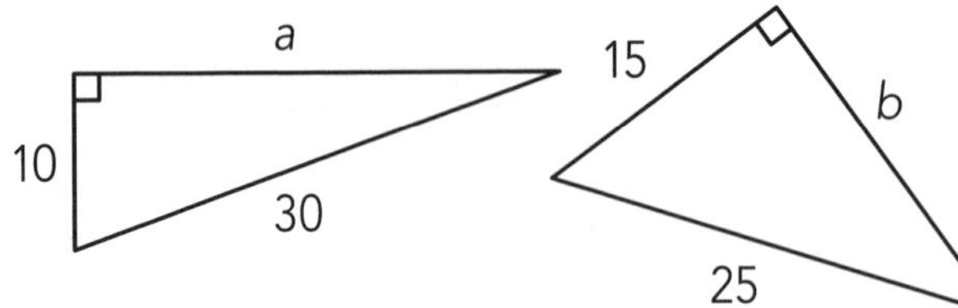

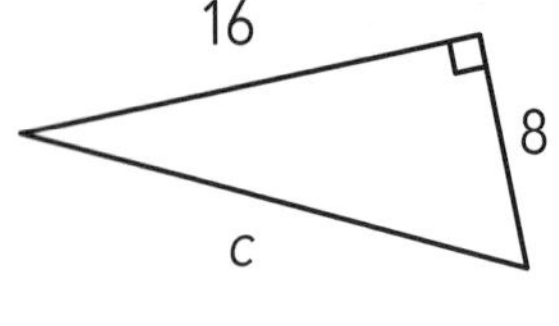

4. a = __________ **5.** b = __________ **6.** c = __________

Applying the Pythagorean Theorem

Triangles

Draw and label sketches if necessary. Round answers to the nearest hundredth.

1. A rectangle has side lengths of 8 cm and 11 cm. Find the length of the diagonal of the rectangle.

____

2. A square has a side length of 5 m. Find the length of the diagonal of the square.

____

3. A square has a diagonal with a length of 10'. Find the length of one side of the square.

____

4. A 40' tall telephone pole is supported with a wire from the top of the pole to the ground. If the wire is attached to the ground at a spot 10' from the pole, how long is the wire?

____

5. To get from home to school, Mindy must walk 0.75 miles east and 0.5 miles north. Determine the straight-line distance from Mindy's house to school.

____

The Converse of the Pythagorean Theorem

You can use the Pythagorean theorem to determine if a triangle is acute, right, or obtuse.

Side lengths:	6, 8, 10	9, 12, 16	7, 8, 6
	$a^2 + b^2 = c^2$	$a^2 + b^2 = c^2$	$a^2 + b^2 = c^2$
	$6^2 + 8^2 = 10^2$	$9^2 + 12^2 = 16^2$	$6^2 + 7^2 = 8^2$
	$36 + 64 = 100$	$81 + 144 < 256$	$36 + 49 > 64$
	right triangle	obtuse triangle	acute triangle

Determine if the three lengths would make an acute, right, or obtuse triangle.

1. 3, 4, 5 ________________

2. 5, 12, 11 ________________

3. 20, 10, 12 ________________

4. 0.7, 2.4, 2.5 ________________

5. 5, 12, 13 ________________

6. 6, 12, 8 ________________

7. 6, 6, 11 ________________

8. 5, 5, 5 ________________

9. 9, 15, 12 ________________

10. 50, 40, 30 ________________

Classifying Quadrilaterals

Quadrilaterals

A **trapezoid** has exactly one pair of parallel sides.

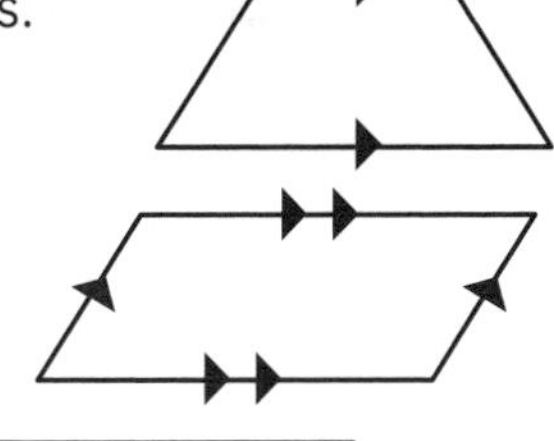

A **parallelogram** has two pairs of parallel sides.

A **rectangle** is an equiangular parallelogram.

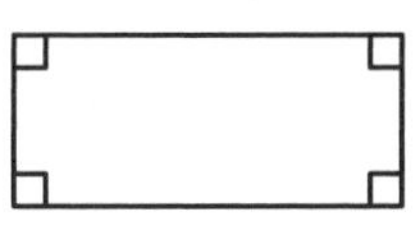

A **rhombus** is an equilateral parallelogram.

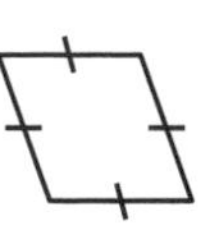

A **square** is both equilateral and equiangular.

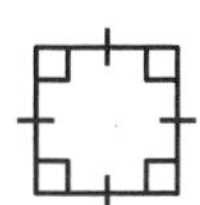

Determine the type of quadrilateral.

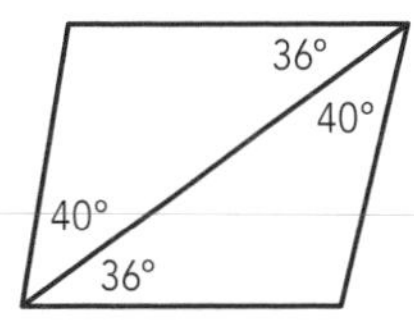

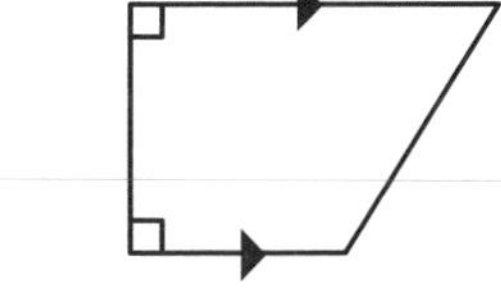

1. ______________________

2. ______________________

5

5 5

5

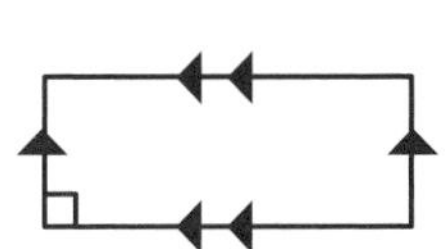

3. ______________________

4. ______________________

120° 120°

60° 60°

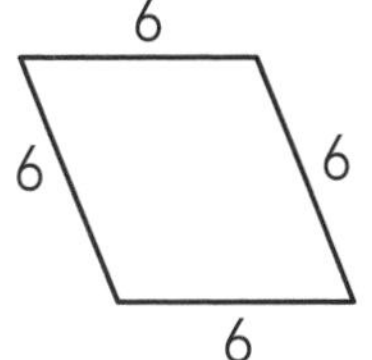

5. ______________________

6. ______________________

Angle Measures of Quadrilaterals

The interior angles of a quadrilateral equal 360°.

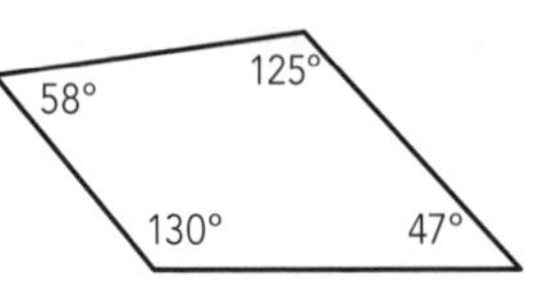

58° + 130° + 47° + 125° = 360°

The opposite angles of a parallelogram are congruent.

The angles between the parallel sides of a trapezoid are supplementary.

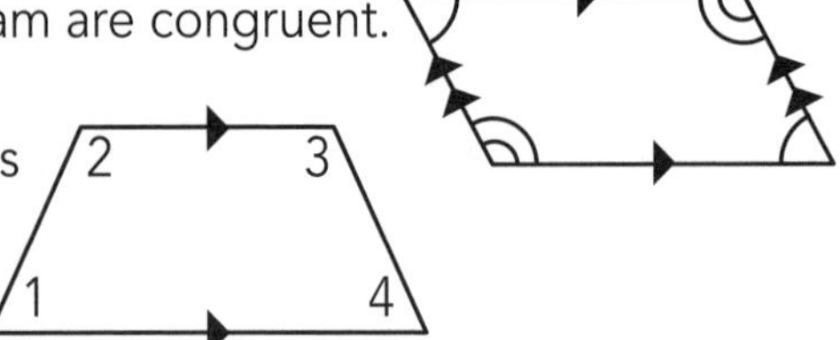

Find the missing angle measures.

1. parallelogram ABCD

m∠A = _____°

m∠B = _____°

m∠D = _____°

A
B
D
64°
C

2. trapezoid WXYZ

m∠W = _____°

m∠Y = _____°

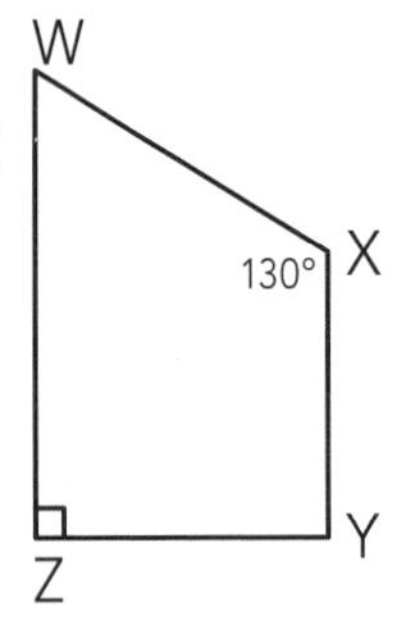

3. quadrilateral MNOP

m∠N = _____°

M
62°
P
67°
170°
N
O

4. rectangle STUV

m∠V = _____°

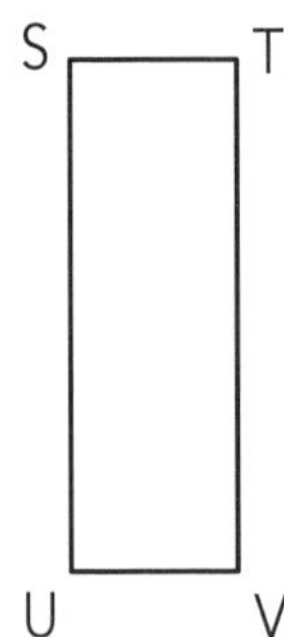

5. trapezoid DEFG

m∠F = _____°

m∠G = _____°

m∠D = _____°

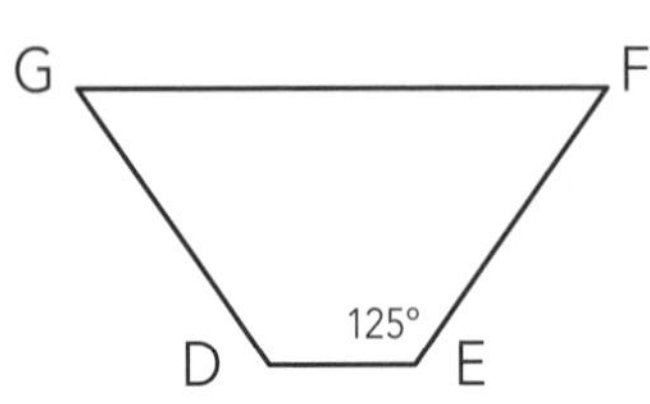

Side Lengths of Quadrilaterals

Quadrilaterals

The opposite sides of a parallelogram are congruent.

All four sides of a rhombus are congruent.

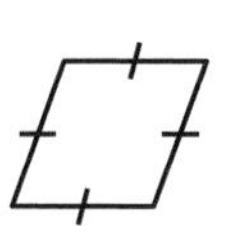

The two legs of an isosceles trapezoid are congruent.

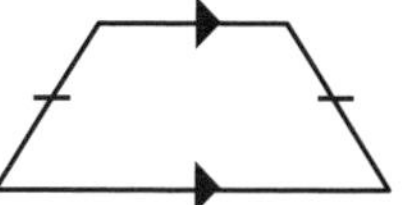

Find the missing side lengths.

1. parallelogram ABCD

$\overline{BC}$ = _____

$\overline{CD}$ = _____

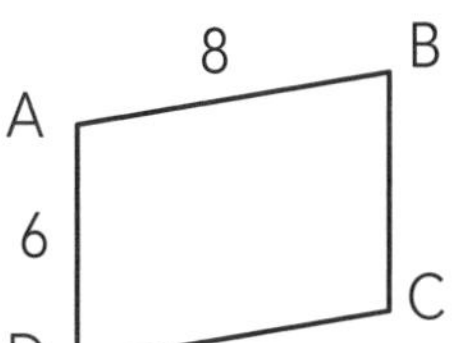

2. rhombus WXYZ

$\overline{WX}$ = _____

$\overline{WZ}$ = _____

$\overline{YZ}$ = _____

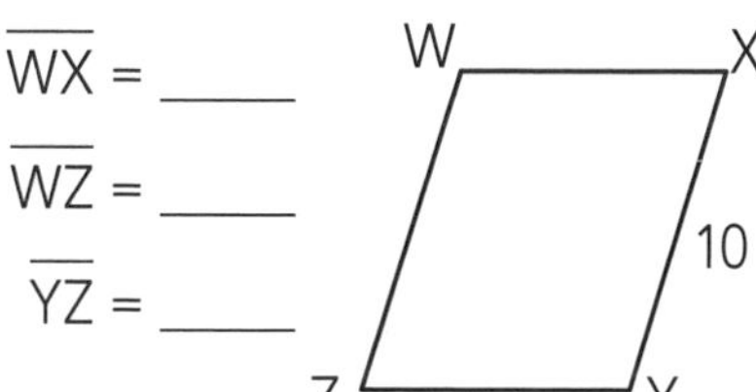

3. isosceles trapezoid MNOP

$\overline{NO}$ = _____

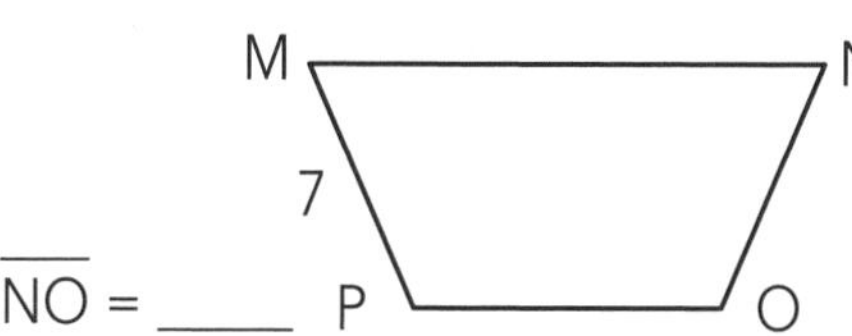

4. rhombus PQRS

$\overline{PQ}$ = _____

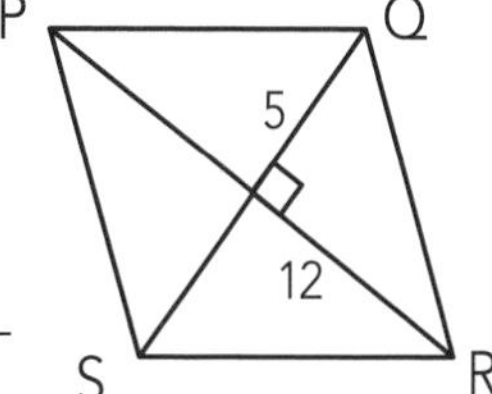

5. parallelogram GHIJ

$\overline{HI}$ = _____

$\overline{IJ}$ = _____

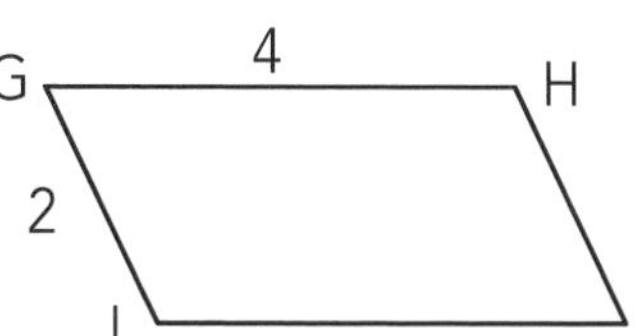

Solving Proportions

A **proportion** shows that two ratios are equal.

To solve a proportion, cross multiply and solve.

$$\frac{10}{8} = \frac{x}{12} \qquad \frac{x}{7} = \frac{3}{5}$$

$10 \bullet 12 = 8x \qquad 5x = 7 \bullet 3$

$120 = 8x \qquad 5x = 21$

$x = 15 \qquad x = \frac{21}{5}$

Solve for x.

1. $\frac{15}{x} = \frac{25}{5}$ x = _____

2. $\frac{5}{7} = \frac{x}{21}$ x = _____

3. $\frac{8}{14} = \frac{6}{x}$ x = _____

4. $\frac{3}{13} = \frac{10}{x}$ x = _____

5. $\frac{1}{6} = \frac{22}{x}$ x = _____

6. $\frac{3}{5} = \frac{x}{35}$ x = _____

Similar Polygons

Similarity

Two polygons are **similar** if their corresponding angles are congruent and their corresponding side lengths are proportional.

$\angle A \cong \angle E$
$\angle B \cong \angle F$
$\angle C \cong \angle G$
$\angle D \cong \angle H$

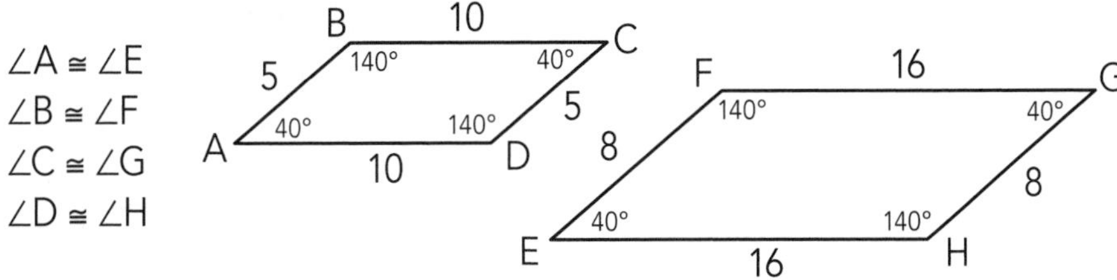

$\frac{AB}{EF} = \frac{BC}{FG} = \frac{CD}{GH} = \frac{AD}{EH} = \frac{5}{8}$ parallelogram ABCD ~ parallelogram EFGH

Determine if each pair of polygons is similar. Circle *yes* if the polygons are similar. Circle *no* if they are not.

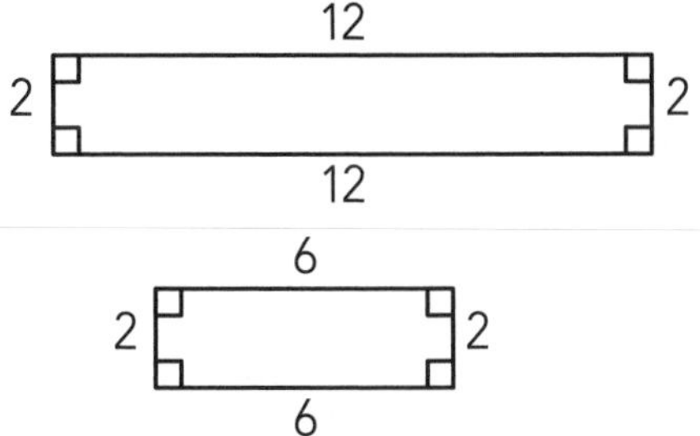

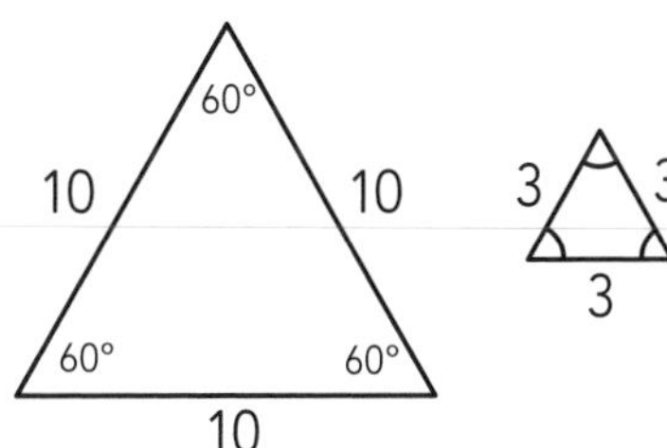

1. Similar? yes no

2. Similar? yes no

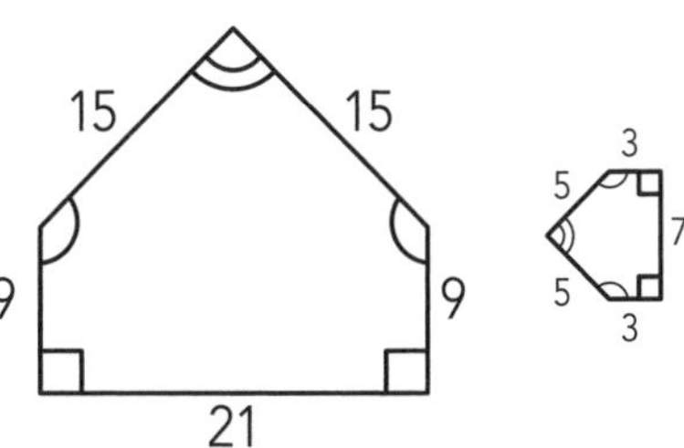

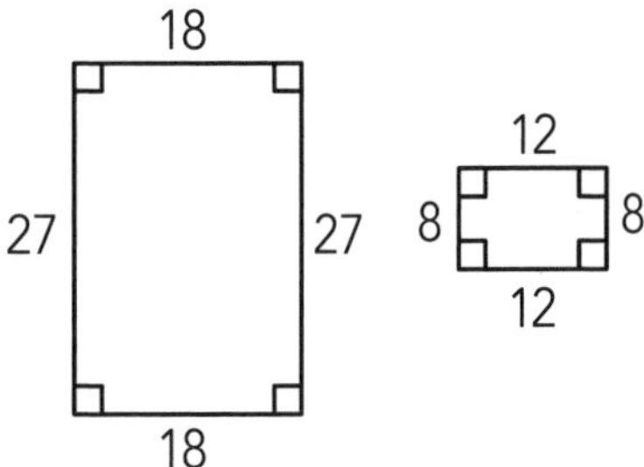

3. Similar? yes no

4. Similar? yes no

5. Are all regular polygons with the same number of sides similar? _____

Similar Triangles

Similarity

Two triangles are similar if:

- Two pairs of corresponding angles are congruent. (**AA**~)

- All three pairs of corresponding sides are proportional. (**SSS**~)

  $$\frac{AB}{DE} = \frac{BC}{EF} = \frac{AC}{DF} = \frac{3}{1}$$

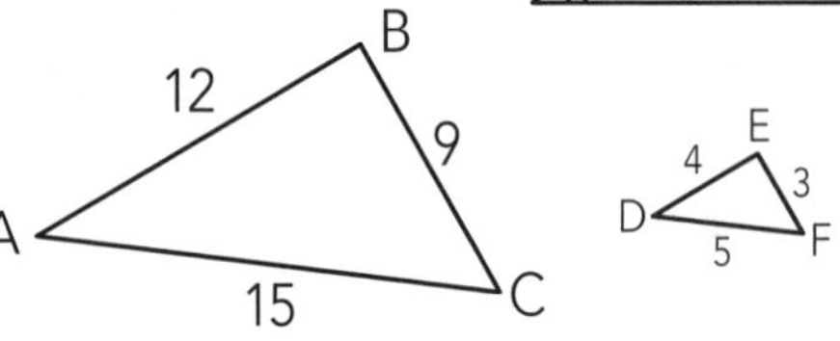

- Two pairs of corresponding sides are proportional, and the included angles are congruent. (**SAS**~)

  $\angle L \cong \angle O$

  $$\frac{JL}{MO} = \frac{KL}{NO} = \frac{2}{1}$$

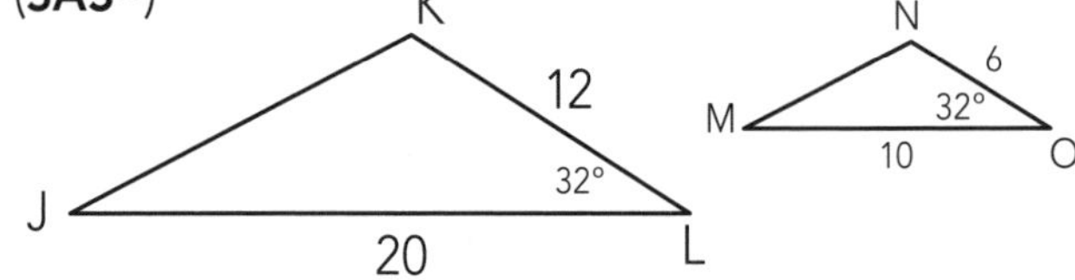

Determine if each pair of triangles is similar. Circle *yes* if the polygons are similar. Circle *no* if they are not. If your answer is yes, state the property that makes them similar.

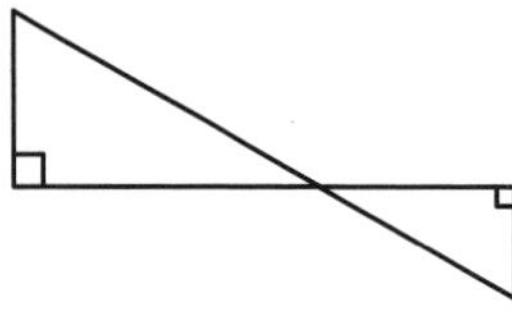

1. Similar? yes no

____

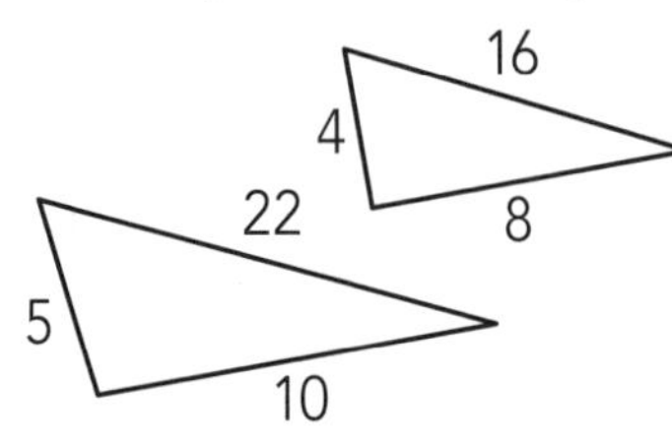

2. Similar? yes no

____

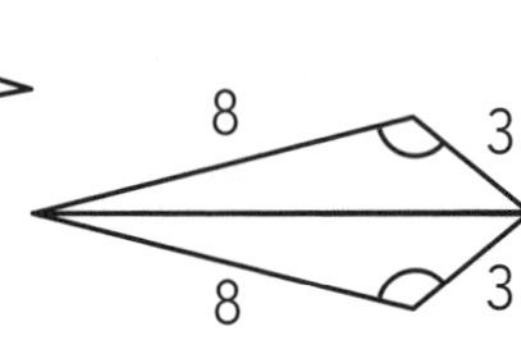

3. Similar? yes no

____

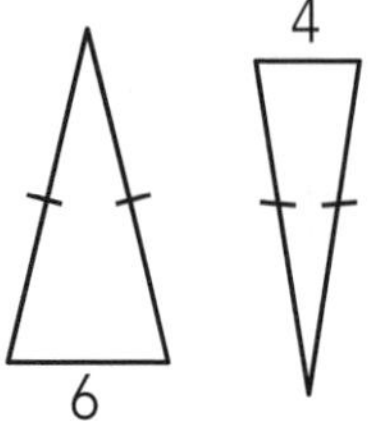

4. Similar? yes no

____

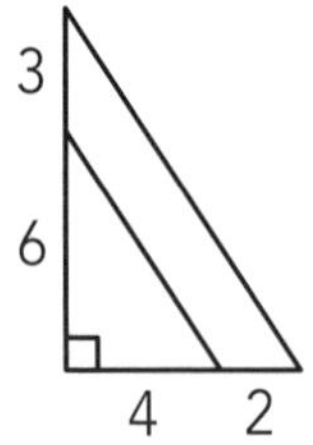

5. Similar? yes no

____

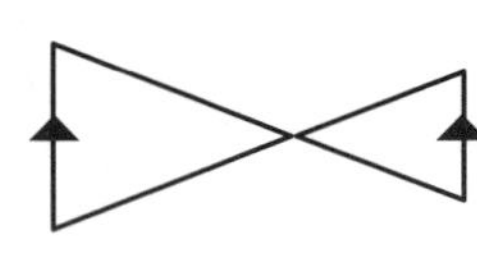

6. Similar? yes no

____

Applying Similarity

Similarity

If two polygons are similar, you can find missing side lengths or angle measures.

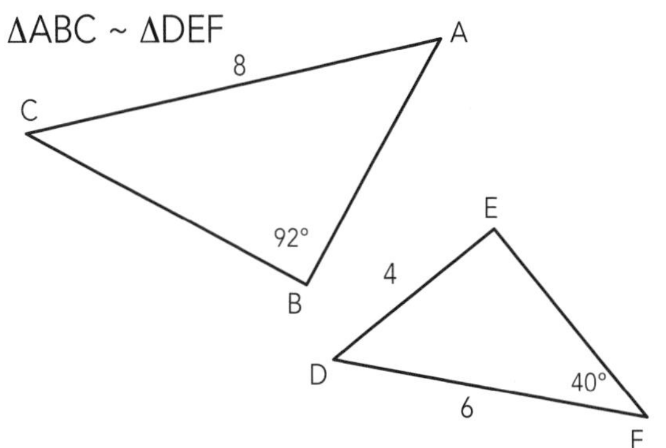

Find $\overline{AB}$

$$\frac{AC}{DF} = \frac{AB}{DE}$$

$$\frac{8}{6} = \frac{AB}{4}$$

$$32 = 6 \bullet AB$$

$$\overline{AB} = \frac{32}{6} = 5\tfrac{1}{3}$$

Find $m\angle C$

$\angle C \cong \angle F$

$m\angle C = 40°$

Find the missing side lengths or angle measures.

pentagon JKLMN ~ pentagon VWXYZ

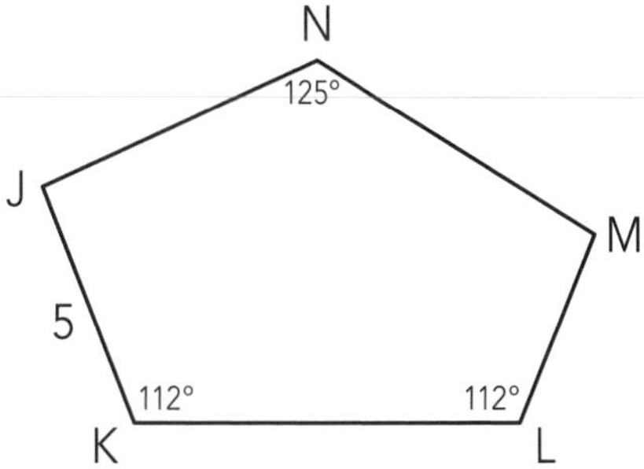

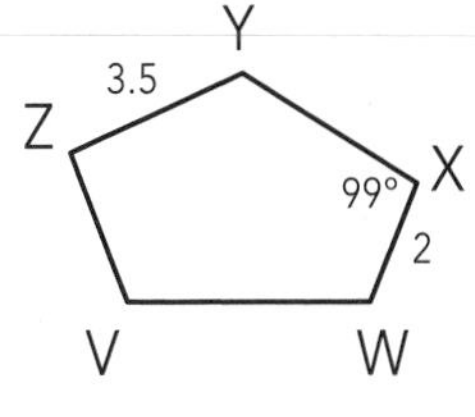

1. m∠M = ________________ °

2. m∠W = ________________ °

3. m∠J = ________________ °

4. m∠Y = ________________ °

5. $\overline{JN}$ = ________________

6. $\overline{KL}$ = ________________

7. $\overline{LM}$ = ________________

8. $\overline{VZ}$ = ________________

Applying Similarity, continued

Use the properties of similar triangles to find each answer. Draw and label a sketch if necessary.

1. A map of Canada has a scale where 2" represents 250 miles. If you measure a distance of 7.5" on the map, determine the number of miles that represents.

____

2. If 1 cm represents 30 km on a map, and Colorado is shown by a rectangle 20 cm long by 15 cm wide, calculate the area of Colorado in square kilometers.

____

3. If a map has a scale of 1 cm to 40 miles, and you take a 500-mile trip, determine how many centimeters you have traveled on the map.

____

4. The blueprints of a rectangular room have a length of 7" and a width of 3". If the actual room is built at a scale of 1" to 5', determine the perimeter of the actual room.

____

Solving Perimeter Problems

Perimeter

The **perimeter** of a polygon is equal to the sum of all of the side lengths.

$P = 10 + 7 + 10 + 7 = 34$

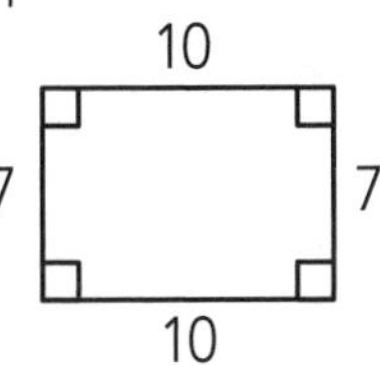

Find the perimeters of the following polygons.

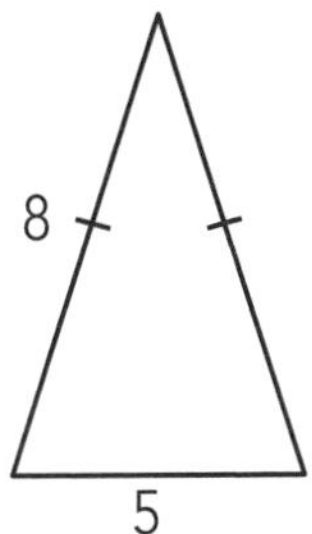

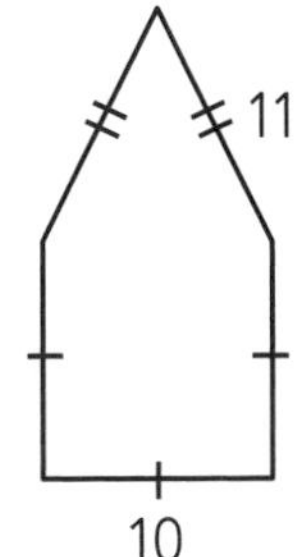

1. P = _______

2. P = _______

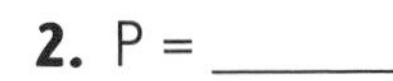

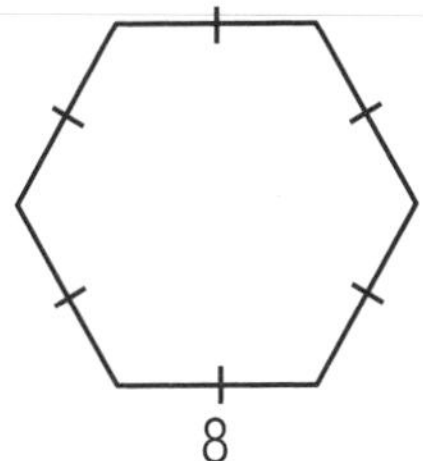

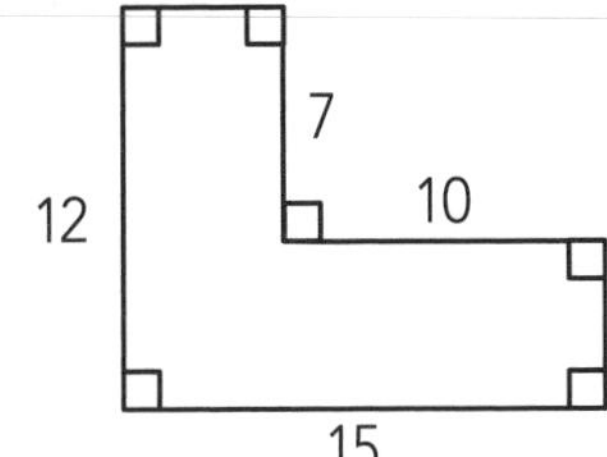

3. P = _______

4. P = _______

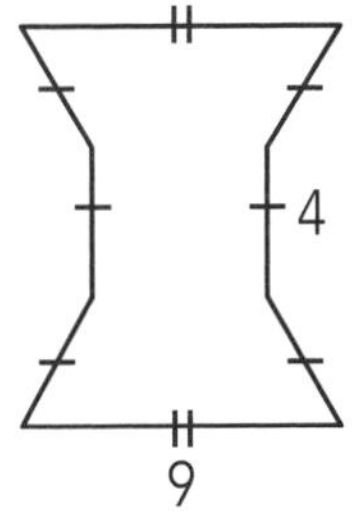

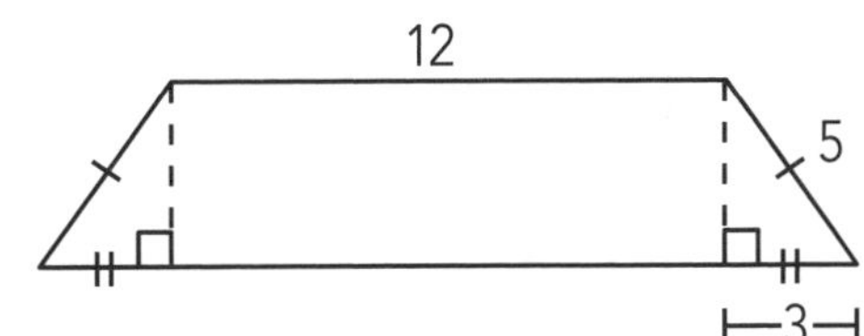

5. P = _______

6. P = _______

Area of Quadrilaterals

To determine the area of a polygon, use the proper formula.

Rectangle: Area = length • width

$A = lw$

$A = 7 \bullet 3$

$A = 21\ \text{cm}^2$

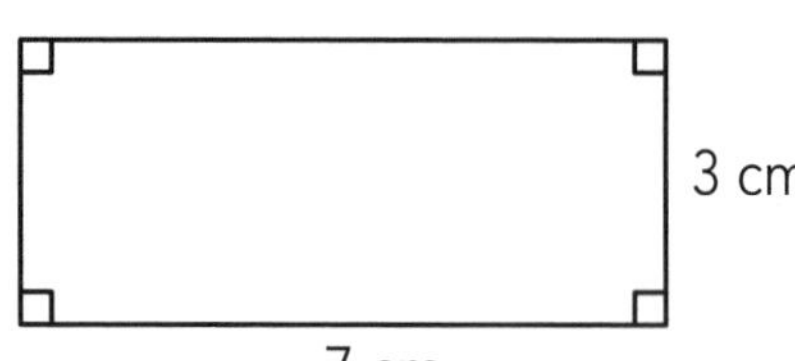

Square: Area = (side length)^2

$A = s^2$

$A = 6^2$

$A = 36\ \text{ft.}^2$

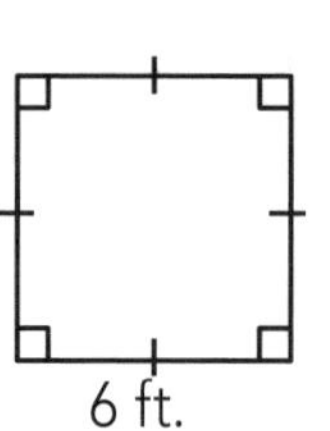

Parallelogram: Area = base • height

$A = bh$

$A = 10 \bullet 6$

$A = 60\ \text{m}^2$

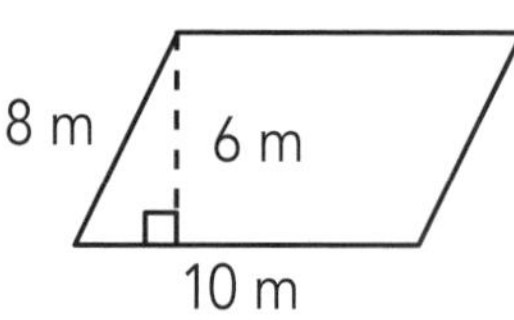

Find the area of each quadrilateral.

square

1. A = ____________

rectangle

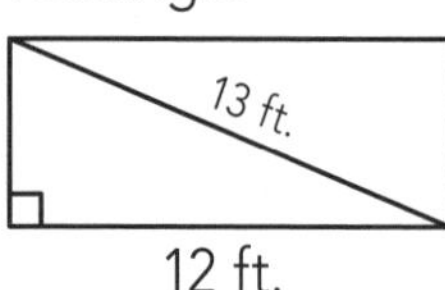

2. A = ____________

parallelogram

5

12

3

3. A = ____________

rectangle

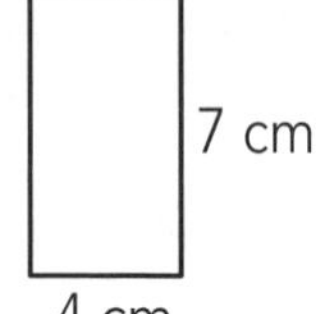

4. A = ____________

square

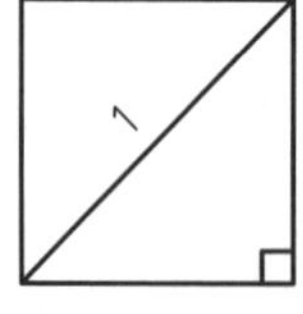

5. A = ____________

parallelogram

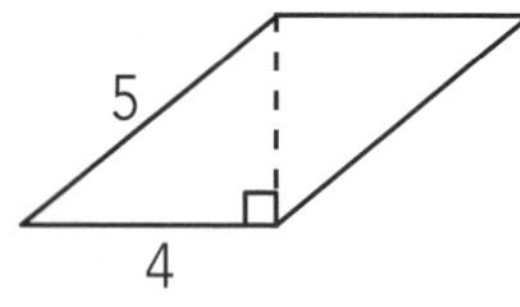

6. A = ____________

Area of Triangles and Trapezoids

Area

To determine the area of a polygon, use the proper formula.

Triangle: Area = $\frac{1}{2}$ • base • height

$A = \frac{1}{2}bh$

$A = \frac{1}{2}(10)(7)$

$A = 35 \text{ in.}^2$

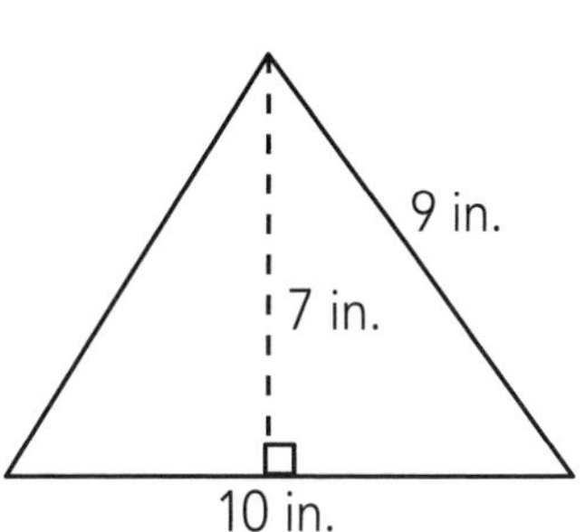

Trapezoid: Area = $\frac{1}{2}$ (sum of the parallel bases) • height

$A = \frac{1}{2}(b + b)h$

$A = \frac{1}{2}(12 + 4)5$

$A = 40$

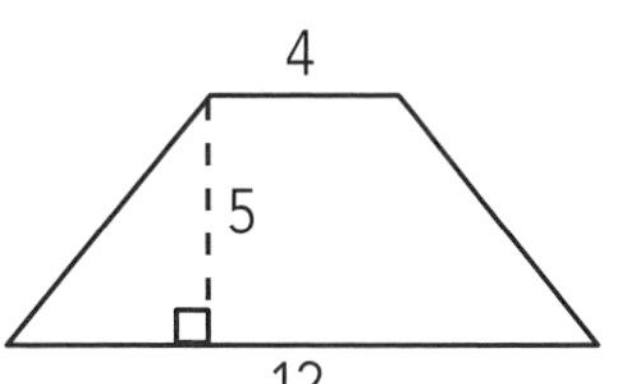

Find the area of each triangle or trapezoid.

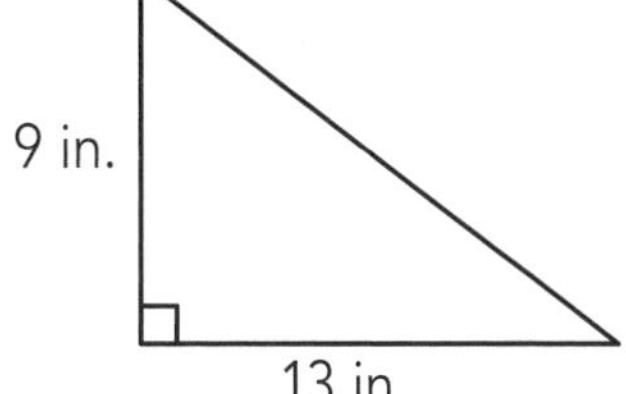

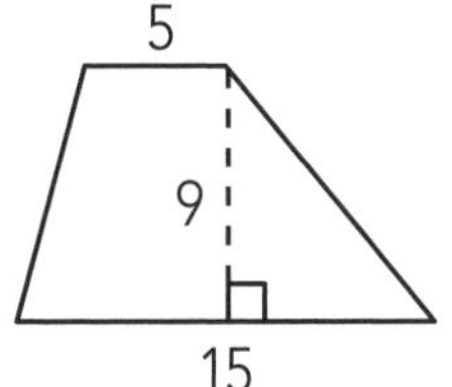

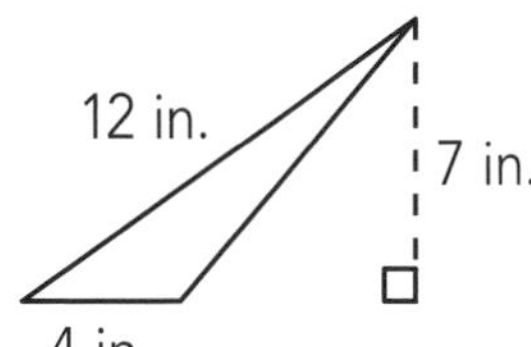

1. A = ____________ **2.** A = ____________ **3.** A = ____________

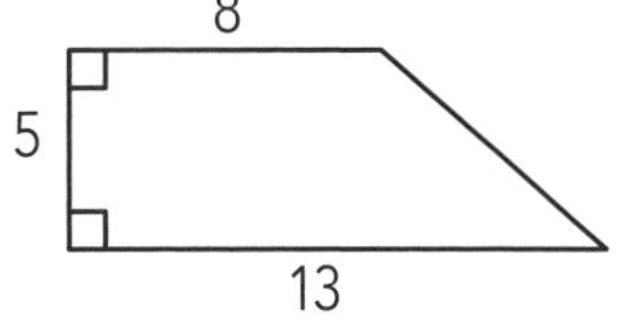

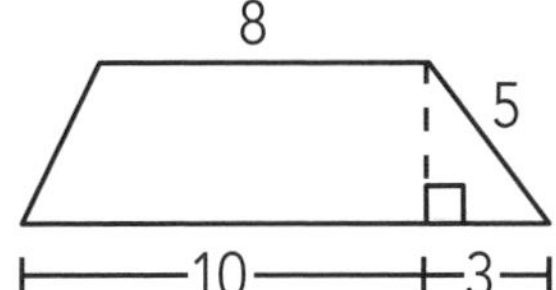

4. A = ____________ **5.** A = ____________

Area of Irregular Shapes

To find the area of an irregular shape, divide it into known polygons.

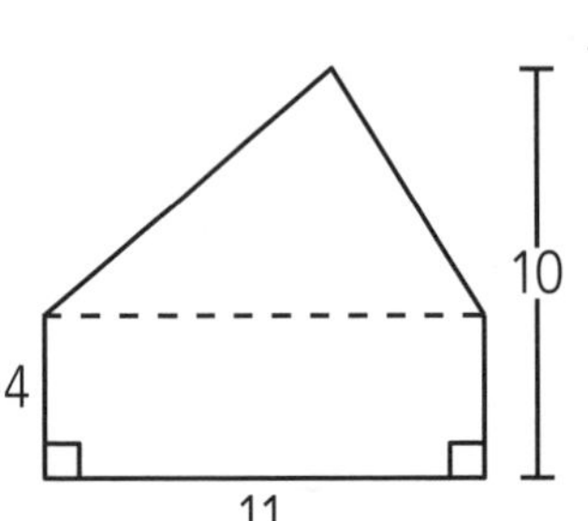

Triangle: $A = \frac{1}{2}bh$ Rectangle: $A = bh$

$A = \frac{1}{2}(11)(6)$ $A = (11)(4)$

$A = 33$ $A = 44$

Total Area = 33 + 44 = 77

Find the area of each irregular shape.

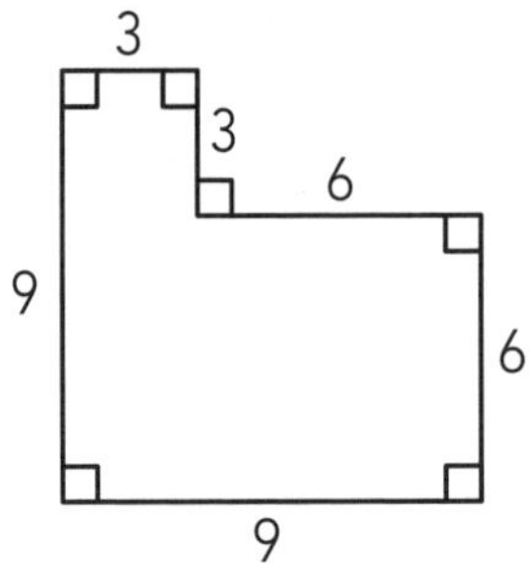

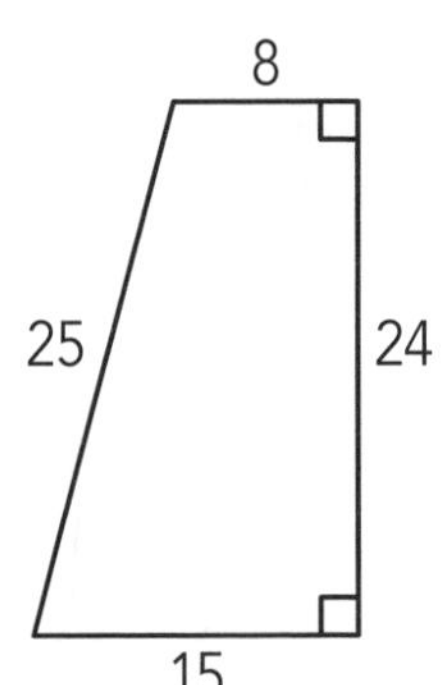

1. A = ______________________

2. A = ______________________

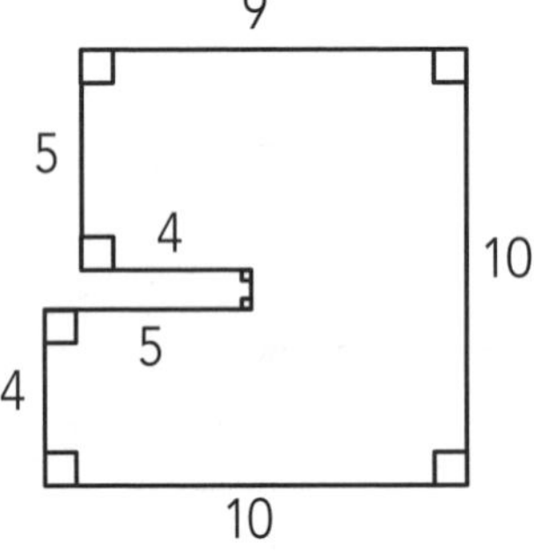

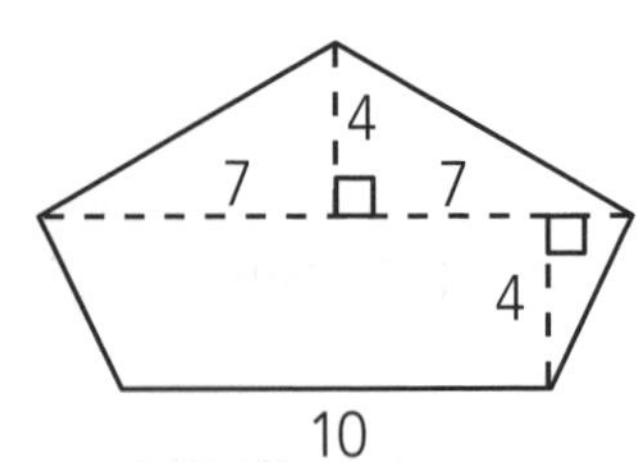

3. A = ______________________

4. A = ______________________

Area of a Shaded Region

Area

The area of a shaded region is equal to the total area of the shape minus the unshaded area.

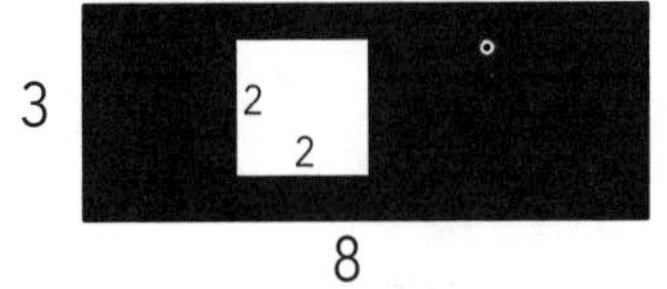

Total Area	Unshaded Area	Shaded Region
$A = bh$	$A = bh$	$A = 24 - 4 = 20$
$A = 8 \bullet 3$	$A = 2 \bullet 2$	
$A = 24$	$A = 4$	

Find the area of each shaded region.

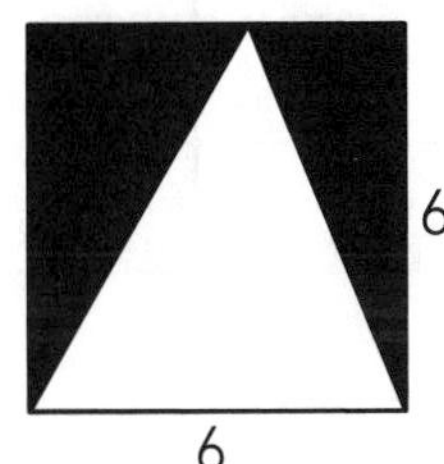

1. A = ____________________

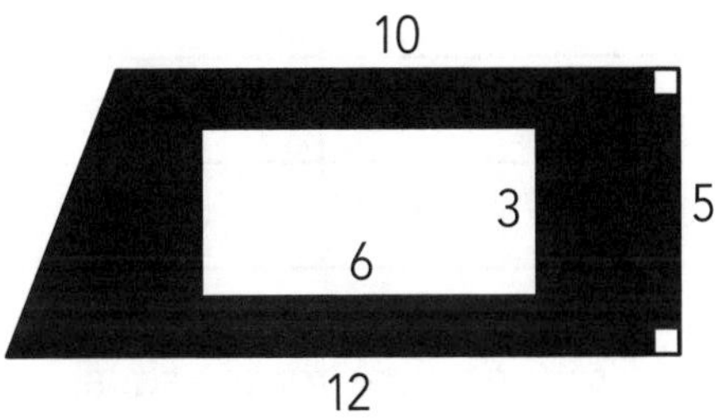

2. A = ____________________

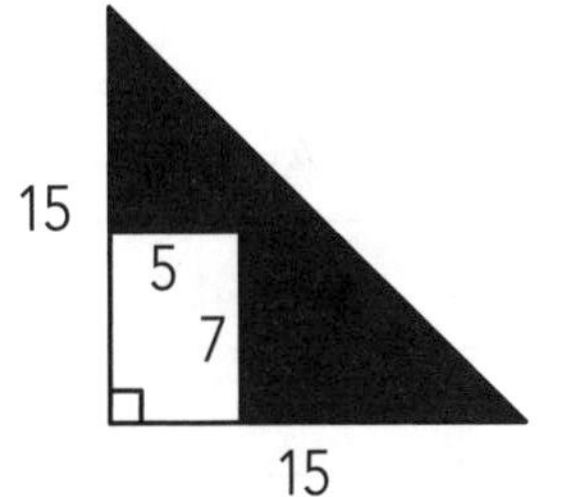

3. A = ____________________

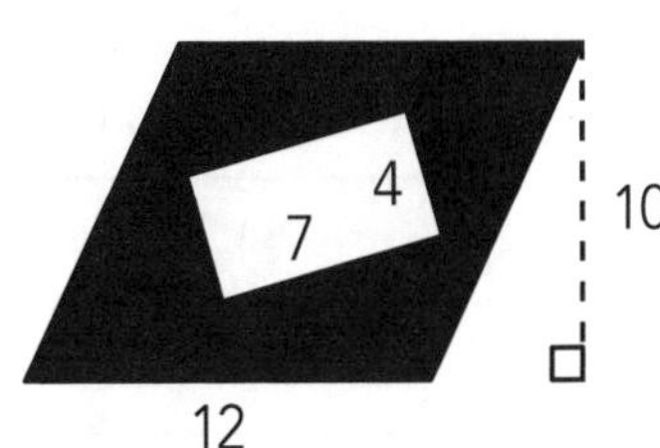

4. A = ____________________

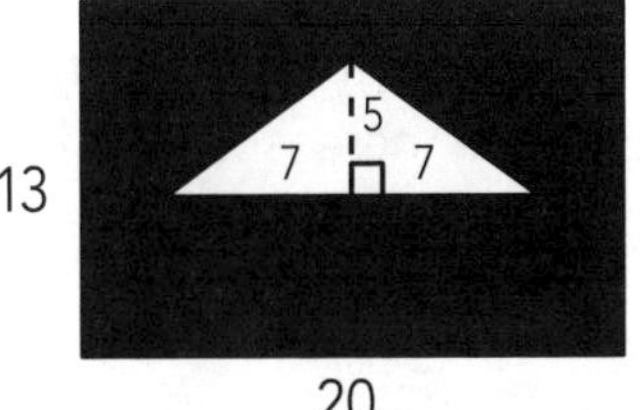

5. A = ____________________

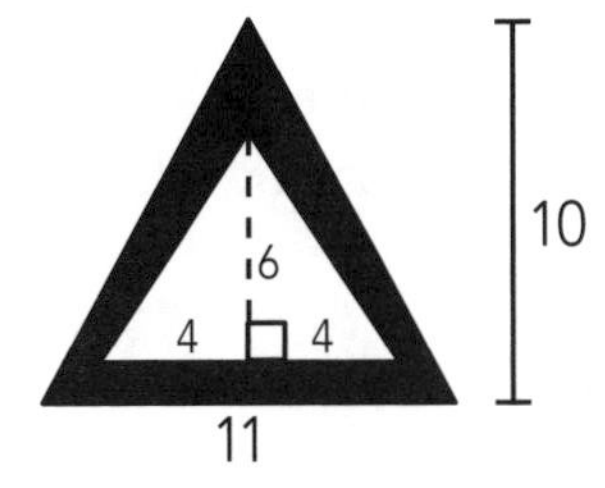

6. A = ____________________

Proportional Perimeter and Area

1. Use the values for the rectangle below to find the perimeter and area.

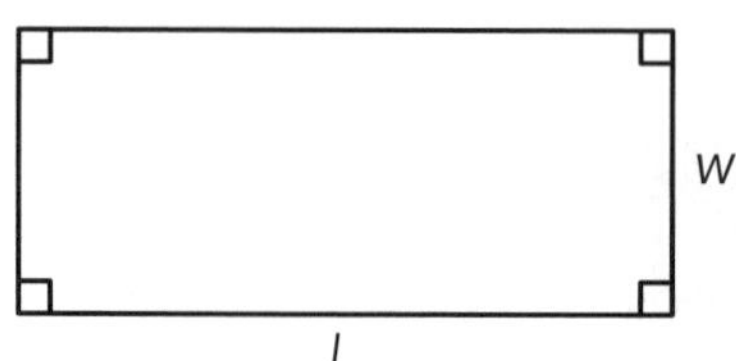

Length (*l*)	Width (*w*)	Perimeter (*P*)	Area (*A*)
3	5		
6	10		
9	15		

2. Use the values for the square below to find the perimeter and area.

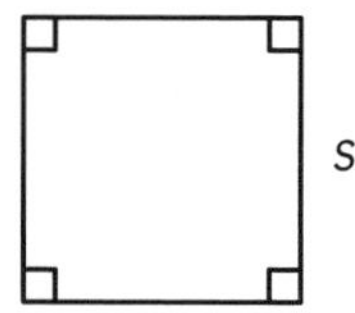

Side Length (*s*)	Perimeter (*P*)	Area (*A*)
1		
2		
3		

Complete the following statements.

3. When the sides of a polygon are doubled in length, the perimeter increases by a factor of _______, and the area increases by a factor of _______.

4. When the sides of a polygon are tripled in length, the perimeter increases by a factor of _______, and the area increases by a factor of _______.

Parts of Circles

Circles

A **chord** is a segment whose endpoints lie on the circle.

The **diameter** is the longest chord of a circle; it passes through the center.

The **radius** of a circle is a segment from the center to the side of the circle.

Circle P

Chord $\overline{AB}$

Diameter $\overline{CD}$

Radii $\overline{CP}$ and $\overline{PD}$

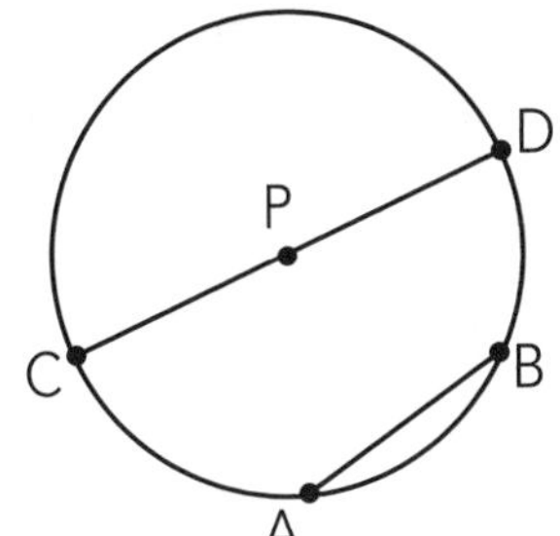

Give all possible answers for each circle part.

1. Chords ______________________________

____

2. Diameters ______________________________

____

3. Radii ______________________________

____

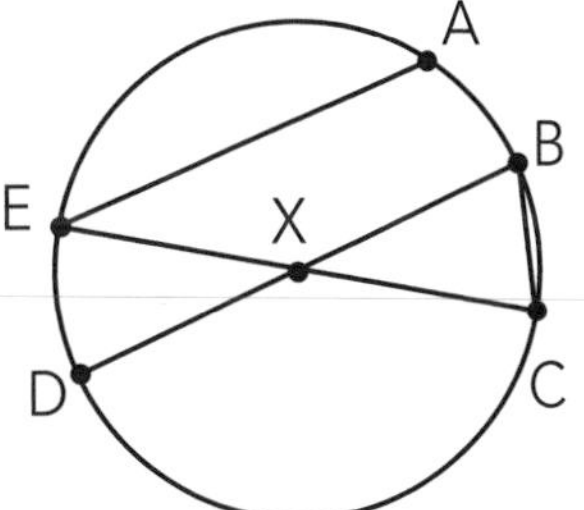

Tell whether each segment is a chord, diameter, radius, or none of these.

4. $\overline{AE}$ ______________ **5.** $\overline{RD}$ ______________

6. $\overline{BC}$ ______________ **7.** $\overline{RA}$ ______________

8. $\overline{BG}$ ______________ **9.** $\overline{FH}$ ______________

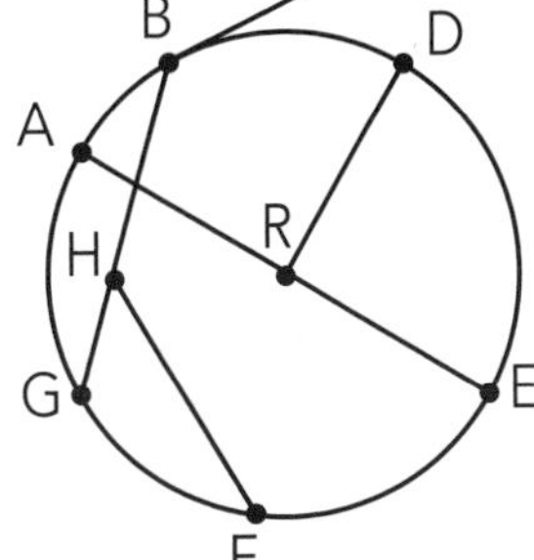

Discovering Pi

1. Measure the circumference, or the distance around a circle, by carefully wrapping a piece of string around each circle and then straightening it out and measuring it with a ruler.
2. Measure the diameter of each circle.
3. Enter both measurements in the table.
4. Divide the circumference by the diameter and write the answer in the last column.

Circle Number	**Circumference** (C)	**Diameter** (d)	$C \div d$
1			
2			
3			
4			
5			
6			

1. 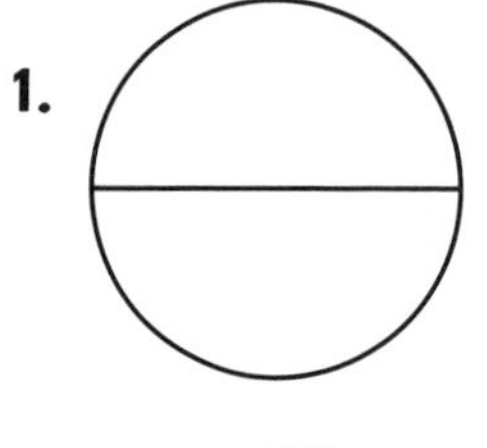

2. 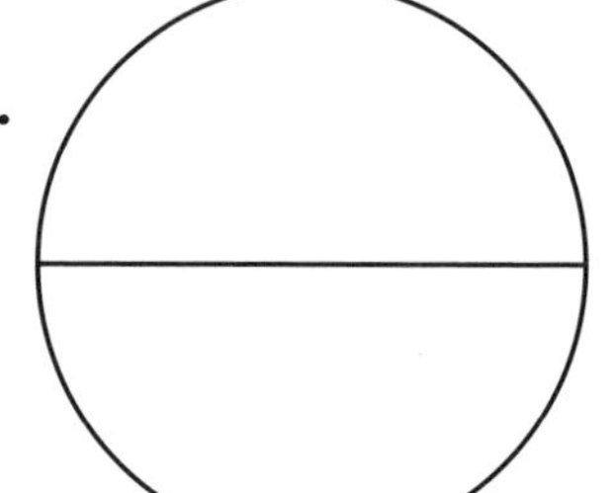

3. 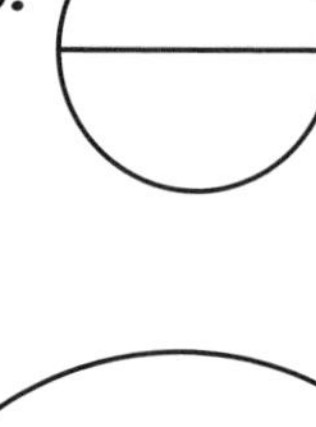

4. 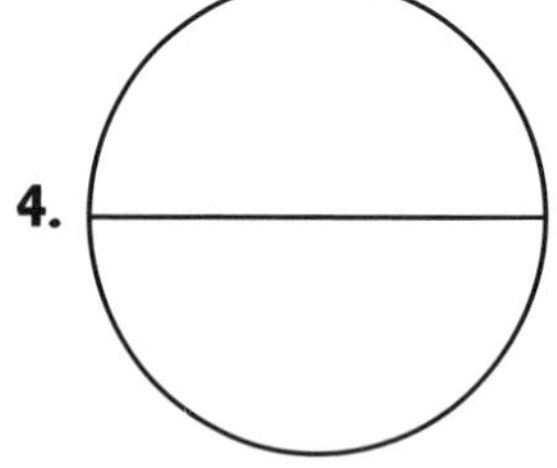

5. 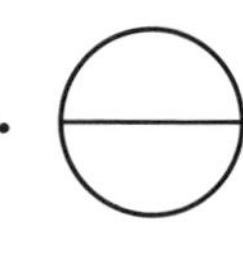

6. 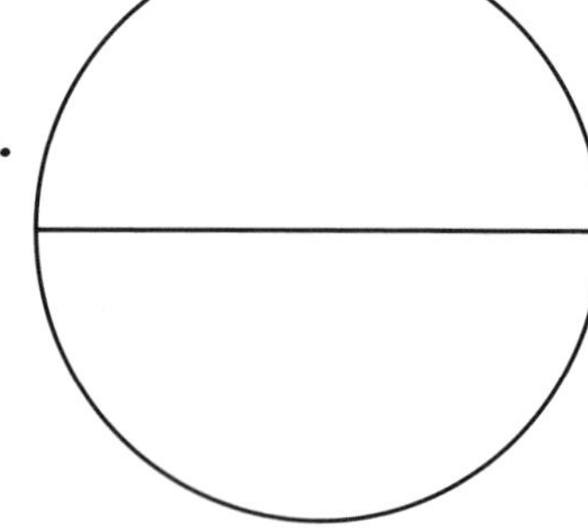

7. Find the average of the "$C \div d$" column entries. ________________

8. **Pi** is the ratio of circumference to diameter: 3.14
Did your answer come close to 3.14? ____________________________

Circumference

Circles

The **circumference** of a circle is the distance around a circle.

To determine the circumference of a circle, use one of two formulas:

Circumference = π • *diameter*

$C = \pi d$

$C = (3.14)(12)$

$C = 37.68$ in.

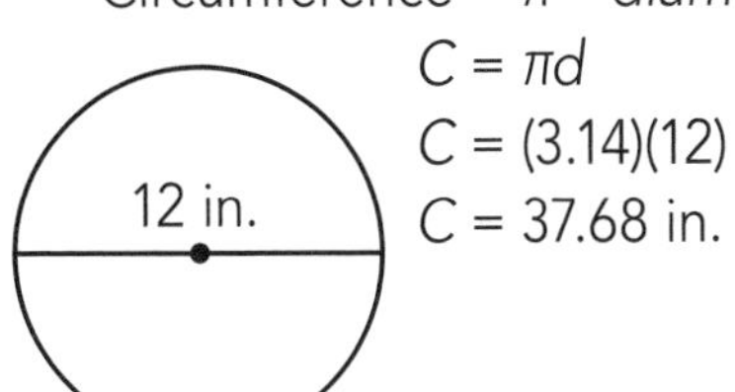

Circumference = 2 • π • *radius*

$C = 2\pi r$

$C = 2\,(3.14)(4)$

$C = 25.12$ cm

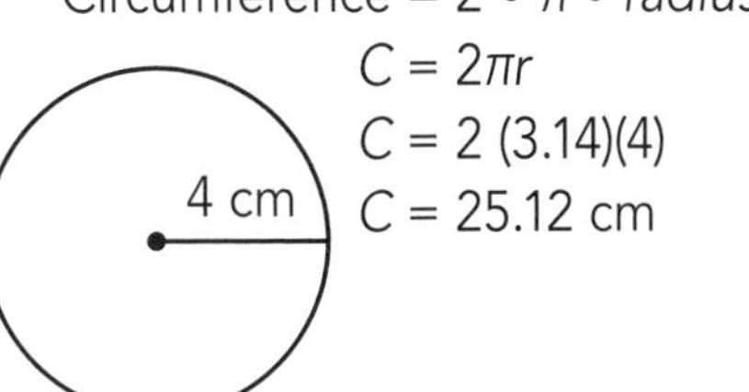

Find the circumference of each circle. Use $\pi = 3.14$.

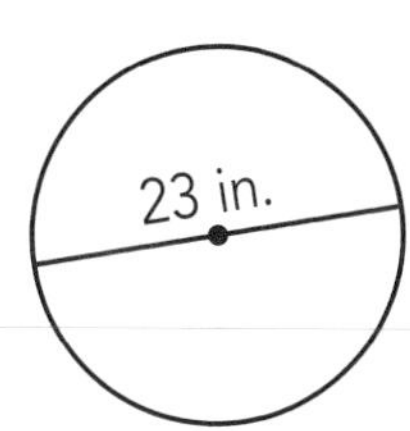

10 m

1. C = ____________________

2. C = ____________________

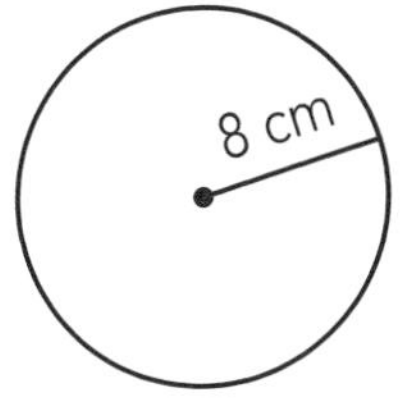

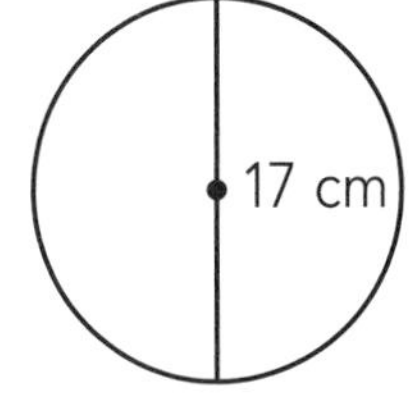

3. C = ____________________

4. C = ____________________

5. A circle has a circumference of 62.8 in. Find the radius of the circle.

____

6. A circle has a circumference of 43.96 cm. Find the diameter of the circle.

____

Area of Circles

The **area** of a circle represents the amount of space in the interior of the circle.

To determine the area of a circle, use the formula: Area = $\pi \bullet (radius)^2$

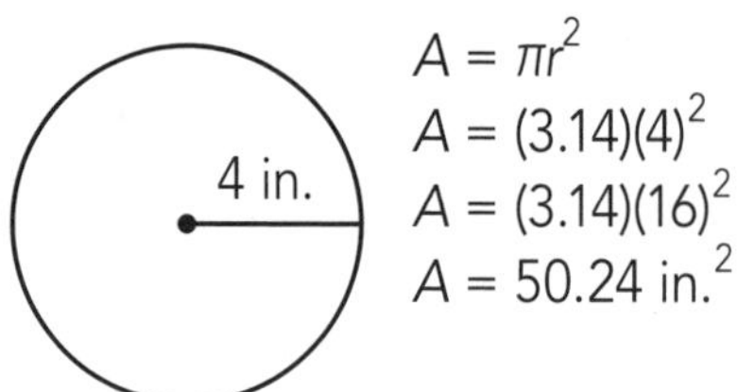

$A = \pi r^2$
$A = (3.14)(4)^2$
$A = (3.14)(16)^2$
$A = 50.24 \text{ in.}^2$

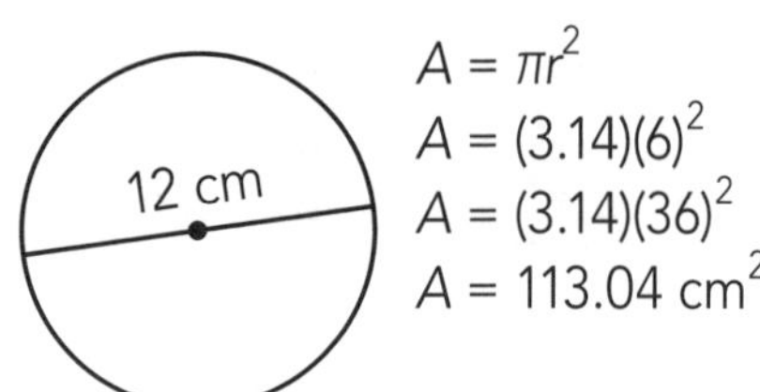

$A = \pi r^2$
$A = (3.14)(6)^2$
$A = (3.14)(36)^2$
$A = 113.04 \text{ cm}^2$

Find the area of each circle. Use $\pi = 3.14$.

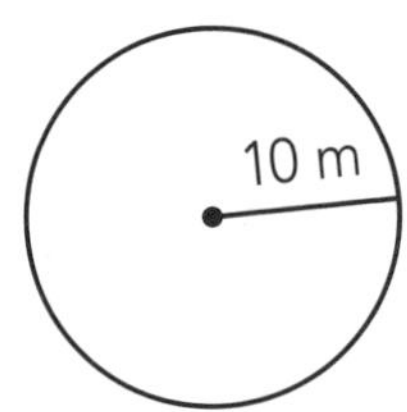

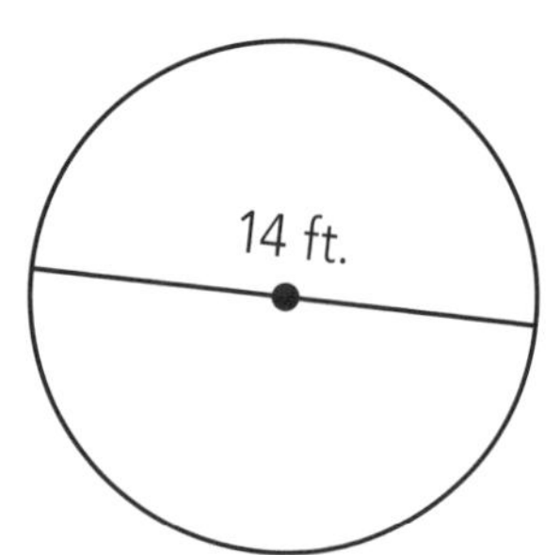

1. A = ______________________ **2.** A = ______________________

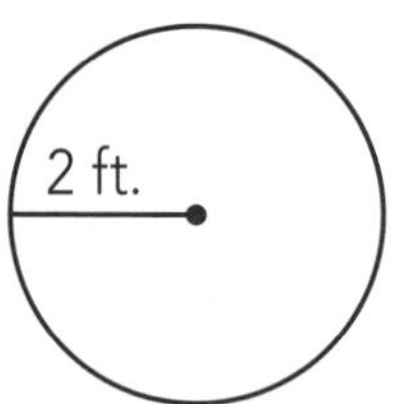

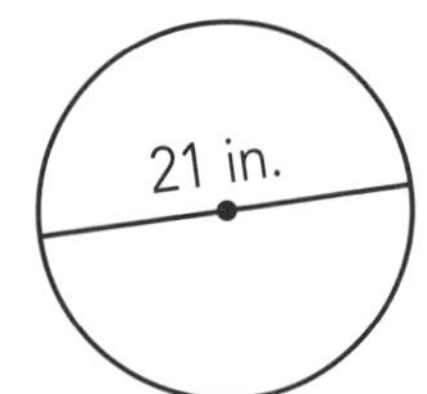

3. A = ______________________ **4.** A = ______________________

5. A circle has a diameter of 9.6 cm. Determine the area of the circle.

____

6. A circle has a circumference of 31.4 cm. Determine the area of the circle.

____

Classifying Solids

Solids

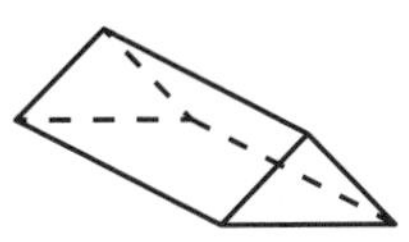

A **prism** is a solid formed by two congruent polygon bases connected by rectangular lateral faces. A prism is named with regard to the polygon bases.

A **cylinder** is a solid formed by two congruent circular bases.

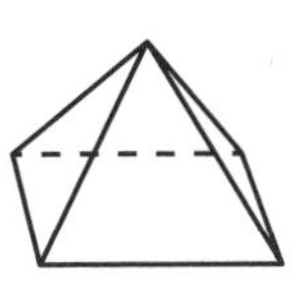

A **pyramid** is a solid formed by one polygon base. The lateral faces are triangles that meet at a vertex. A pyramid is named with regard to the polygon base.

A **cone** is a solid formed by one circular base with a vertex at the opposite end.

Determine whether each given solid is a prism, cylinder, pyramid, or cone.

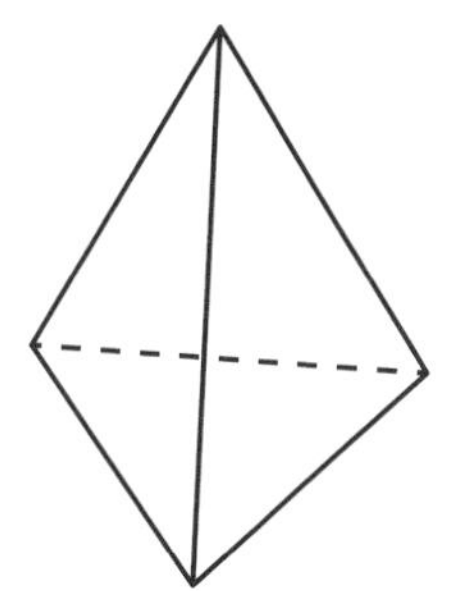

1. ______________________

2. ______________________

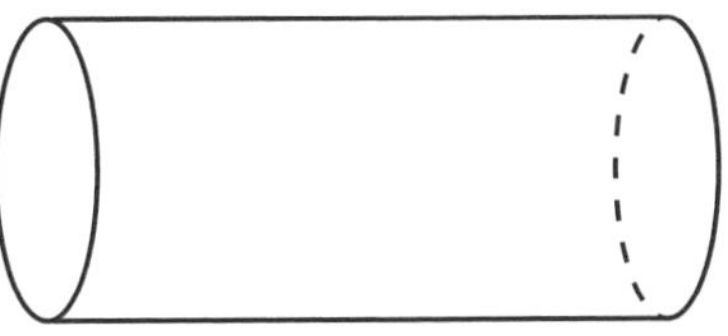

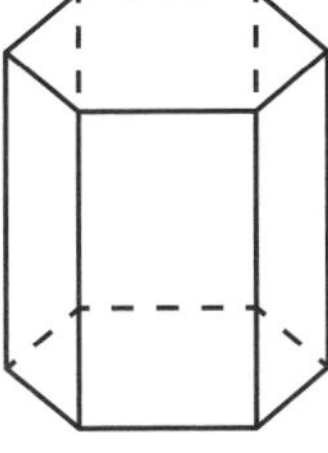

3. ______________________

4. ______________________

Drawing Solids

Draw each solid.

1. a rectangular prism
2. a cylinder
3. a triangular pyramid
4. a cone
5. a pentagonal prism
6. a pentagonal pyramid

Parts of a Prism

Solids

The **vertices** of a prism are the points of intersection.

The **edges** of a prism are the line segments that connect the vertices.

The **faces** of a prism are the planes that make up the sides.

A **cube** (rectangular prism) has 8 vertices, 12 edges, and 6 faces.

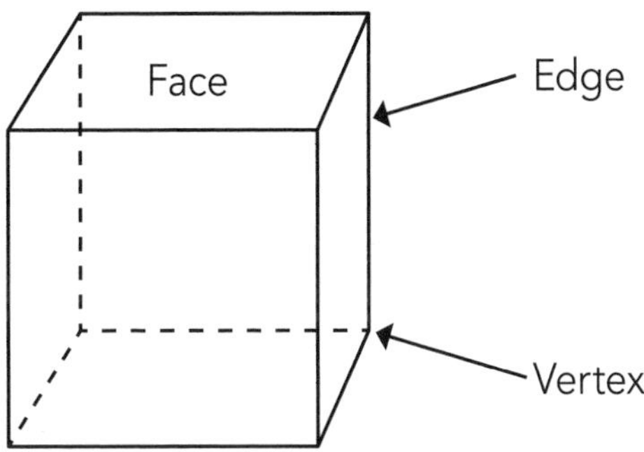

Fill in the following chart. Draw each prism if necessary.

	Type of Prism	Number of Vertices	Number of Edges	Number of Faces
1.	Triangular			
2.	Pentagonal			
3.	Hexagonal			
4.	Heptagonal			
5.	Octagonal			

6. Using your answers from the above chart, try to make predictions regarding the number of vertices, edges, and faces for any size prism. If a prism has polygon bases with *x* number of sides, then the prism has:

_______ vertices, _______ edges, and _______ faces.

Viewing Solids from Different Perspectives

Solid objects can be viewed as two-dimensional objects from different perspectives.

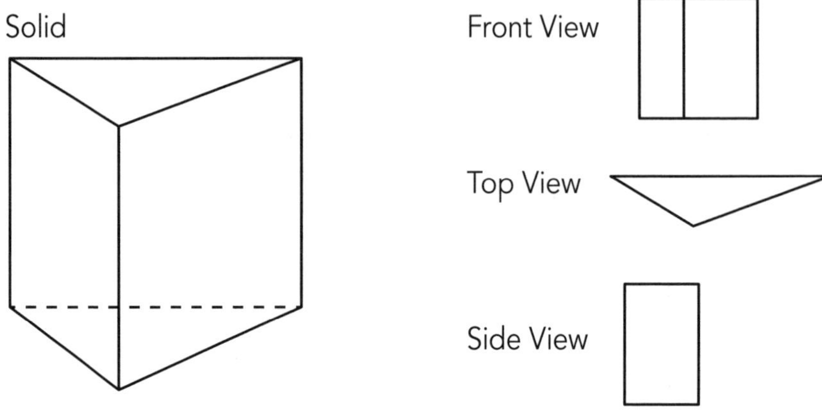

Draw the front view, top view, and side view for each solid.

1.

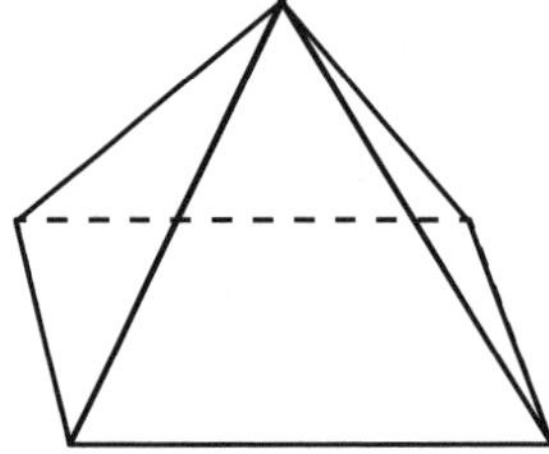

2.

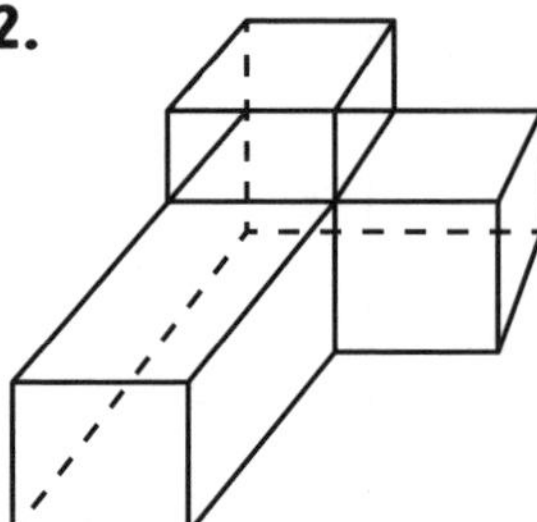

Viewing Solids from Different Perspectives, cont.

Solids

Solids can be drawn when given different perspective views.

Front View 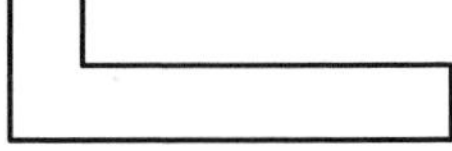

Top View 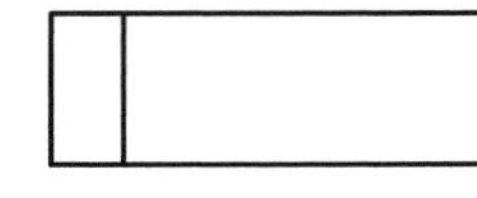

Side View

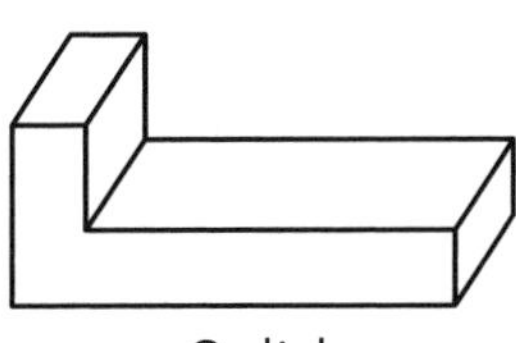

Solid

Given three perspective views, draw each solid.

1. Front view:

Top view:

Side view:

Solid:

2. Front view:

Top view:

Side view:

Solid:

Nets

Solids

A **net** is a two-dimensional figure that represents an unfolded three-dimensional solid.

Solid

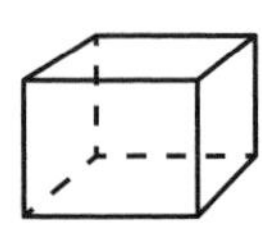

Net

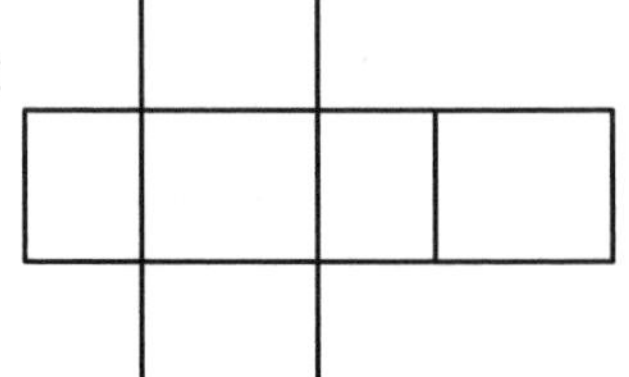

When you draw a net, every face of the solid should be represented. Draw the net for each solid.

1.

2. 

3.

4. 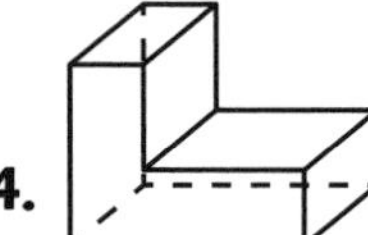

Name the type of solid each net represents.

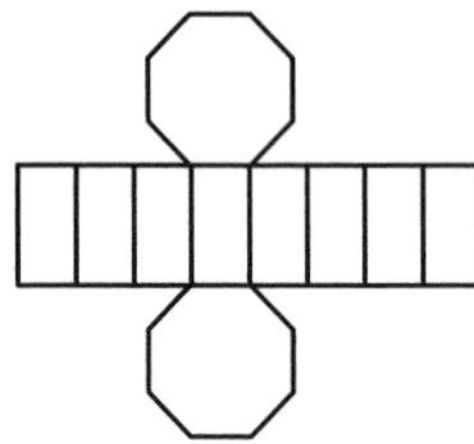

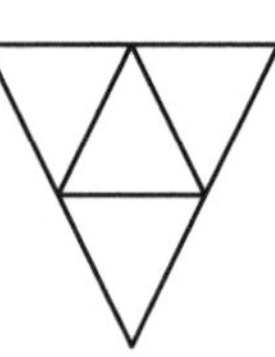

5. ______________________

6. ______________________

Surface Area of a Prism

Solids

The **height of a prism** is the distance between the two bases.

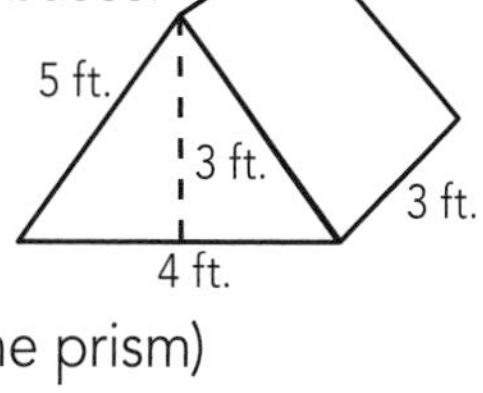

To find the surface area of a prism:

- Find the area of the lateral faces.

  Lateral Area = (perimeter of the base) • (height of the prism)

  $L = Ph$

  $L = (5 + 4 + 5) \bullet 3$

  $L = 14 \bullet 3 = 42 \text{ ft.}^2$

- Find the area of the base (B) using the appropriate formula.

  $B = \frac{1}{2}bh$

  $B = \frac{1}{2}(4)(3)$

  $B = 6 \text{ ft.}^2$

- Combine together using the formula.

  Surface Area = Lateral Area + 2 (area of one base)

  $SA = L + 2B$

  $SA = 42 + 2\,(6)$

  $SA = 54 \text{ ft.}^2$

Find the surface area of each prism.

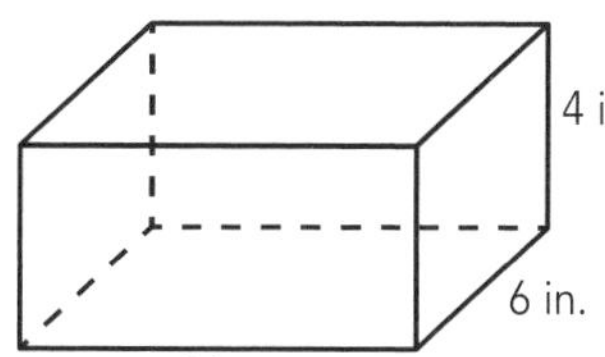

1. SA = ______________________

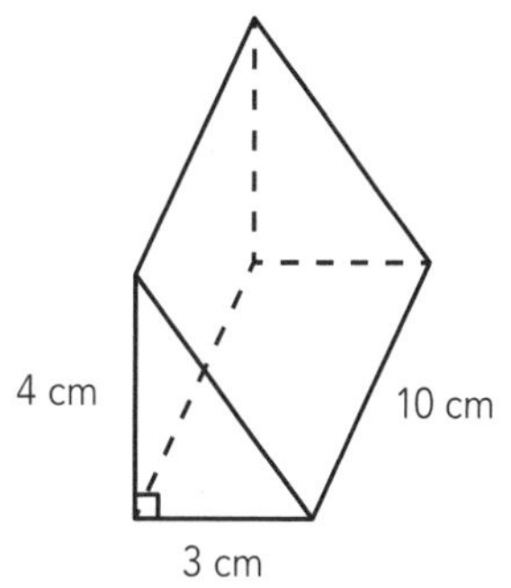

2. SA = ______________________

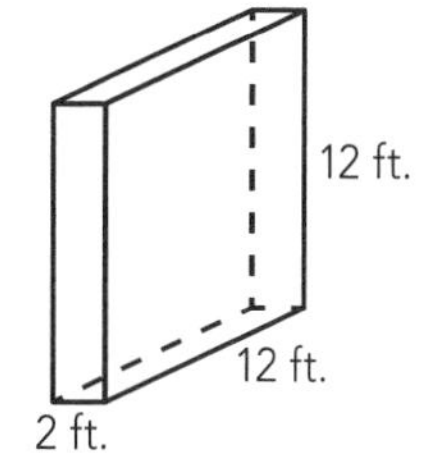

3. SA = ______________________

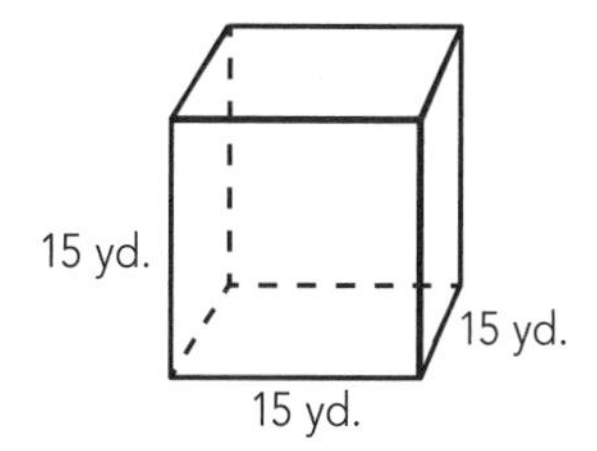

4. SA = ______________________

Volume of a Prism

To find the volume of a prism, use the following formula:
Volume = (area of one base) • (height of the prism)

$B = \frac{1}{2}bh$

$B = \frac{1}{2}(13)(6)$

$B = 39 \text{ in.}^2$

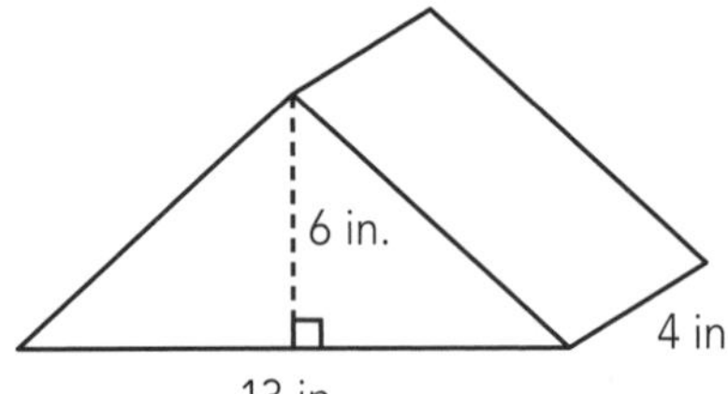

$V = Bh$

$V = (39)(4)$

$V = 156 \text{ in.}^3$

Find the volume of each prism.

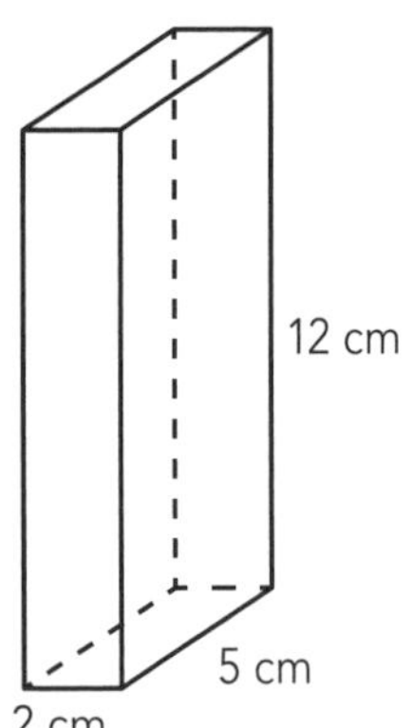

1. V = ____________

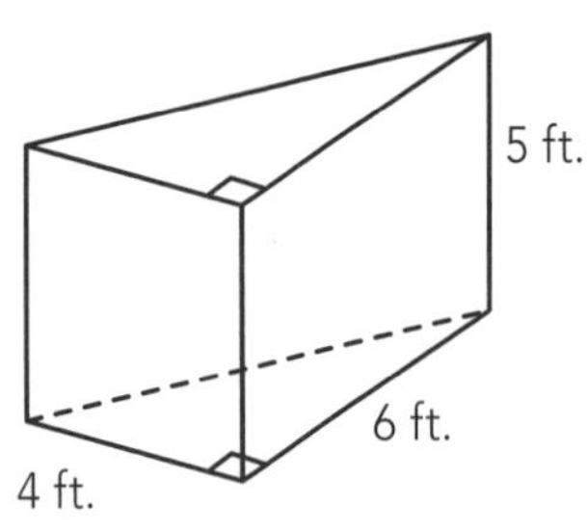

8 m

5 m

3 m

2. V = ____________

3. V = ____________

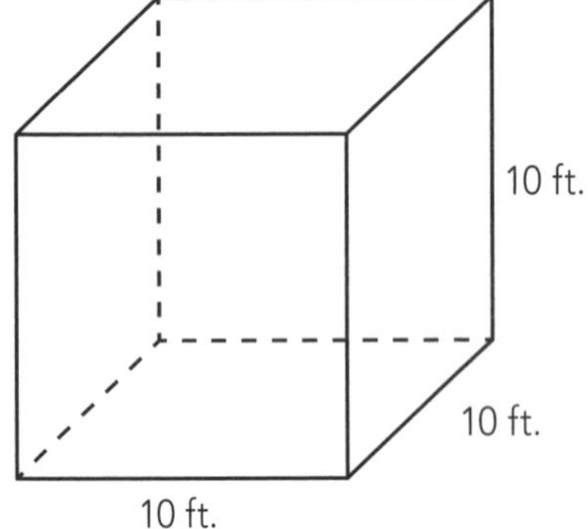

4. V = ____________

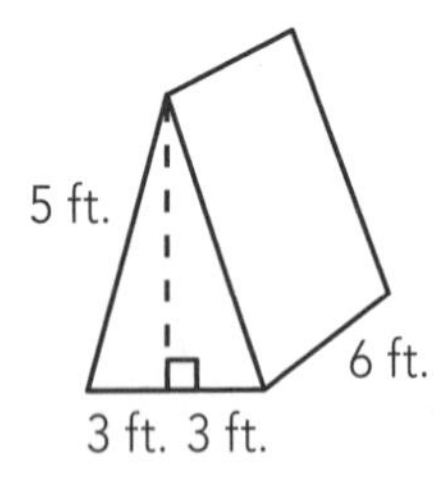

5. V = ____________

Surface Area of a Cylinder

Solids

The **height of a cylinder** is the distance between the two bases. To find the surface area of a cylinder, use the following formula:

Surface Area = 2 (area of the base) + (circumference of the base) • (height of the cylinder)

10 in.

2 in.

$SA = 2\pi r^2 + 2\pi rh$

$SA = 2\,(3.14)(2)^2 + 2\,(3.14)(2)(10)$

$SA = 150.72 \text{ in.}^2$

Find the surface area of each cylinder. Use $\pi = 3.14$.

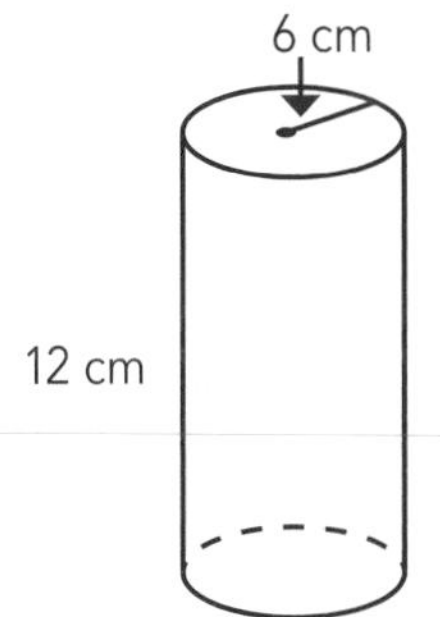

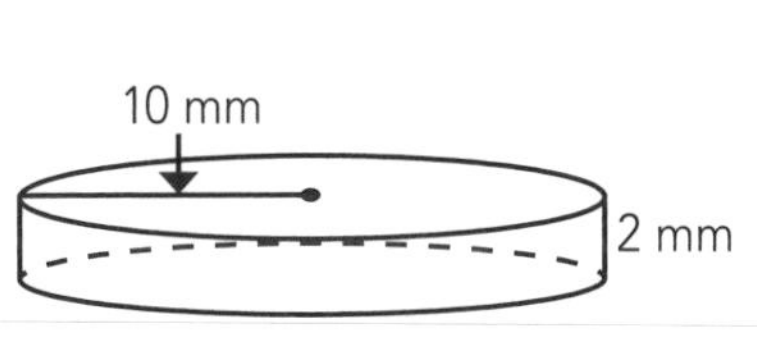

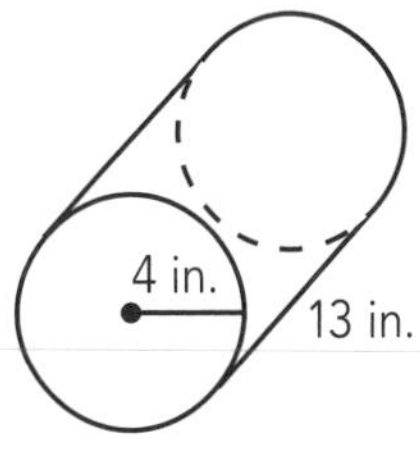

1. SA = __________ **2.** SA = __________ **3.** SA = __________

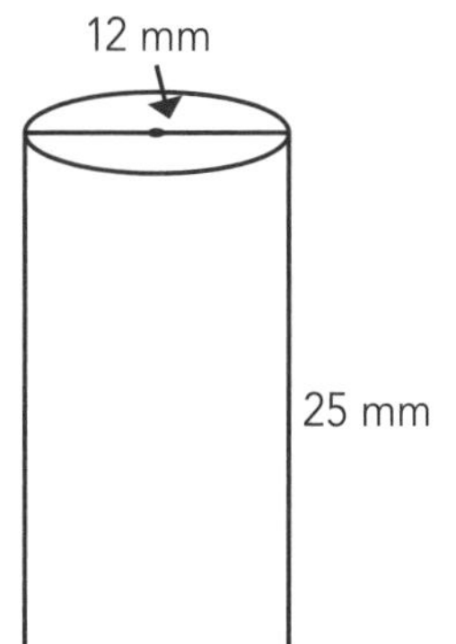

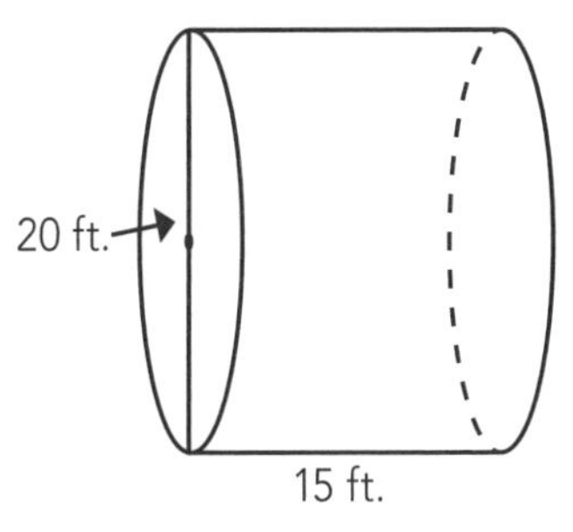

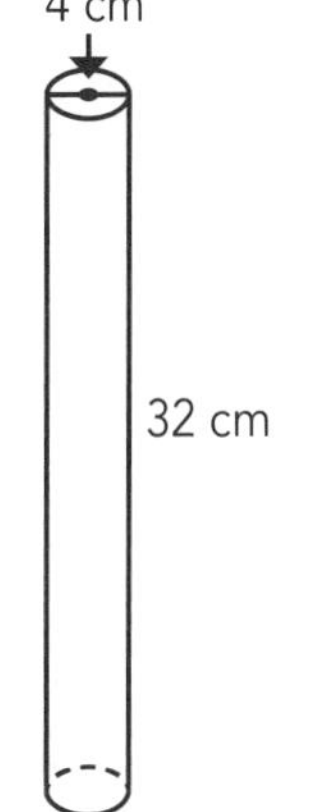

4. SA = __________ **5.** SA = __________ **6.** SA = __________

Volume of a Cylinder

To find the **volume of a cylinder**, use the following formula:

Volume = (area of the base) • (height of the cylinder)

$V = \pi r^2 h$

$V = (3.14)(2)^2(10)$

$V = 125.6 \text{ in.}^3$

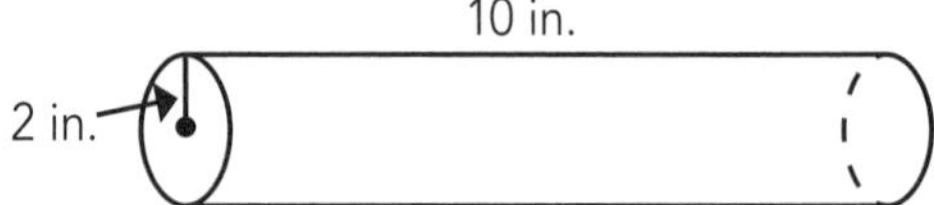

Find the volume of each cylinder. Use $\pi = 3.14$.

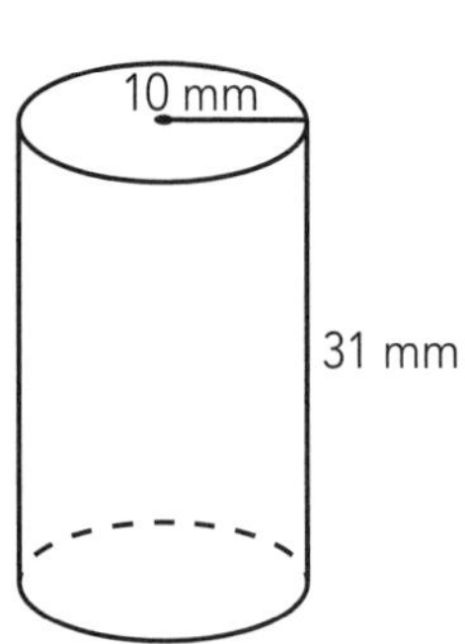

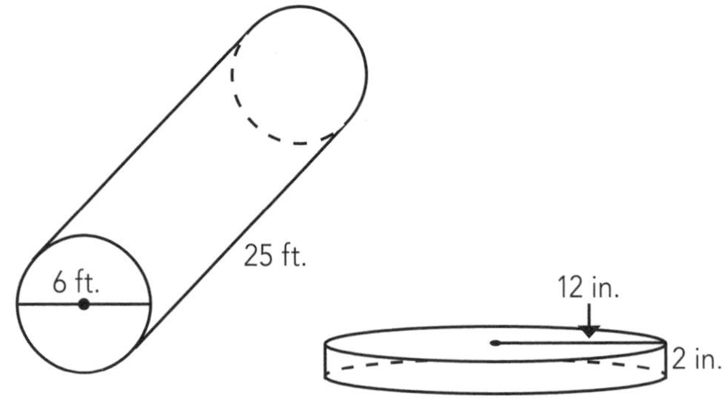

1. V = ____________ **2.** V = ____________ **3.** V = ____________

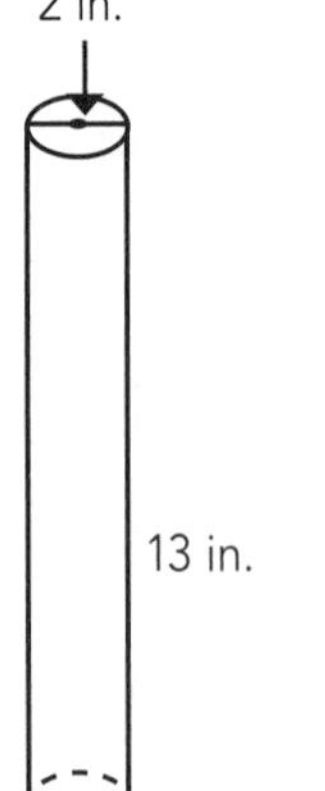

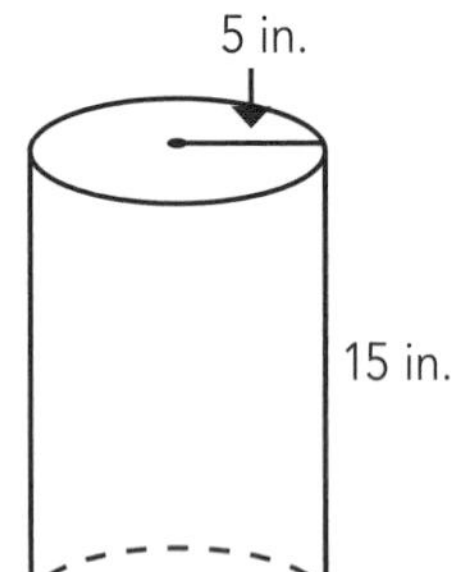

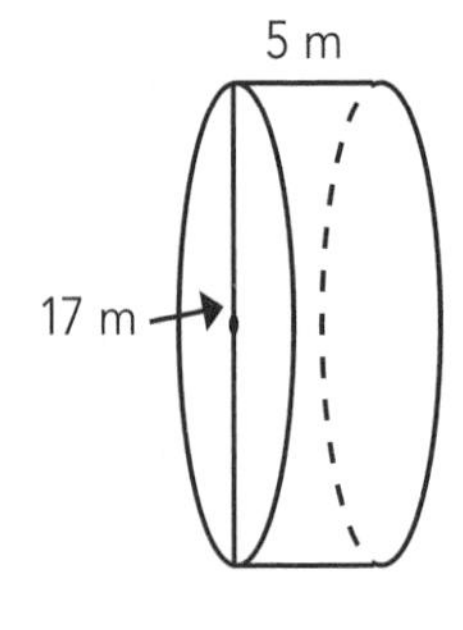

4. V = ____________ **5.** V = ____________ **6.** V = ____________

Surface Area Practice

Solids

Find the surface area of each solid. Use $\pi = 3.14$ when necessary.

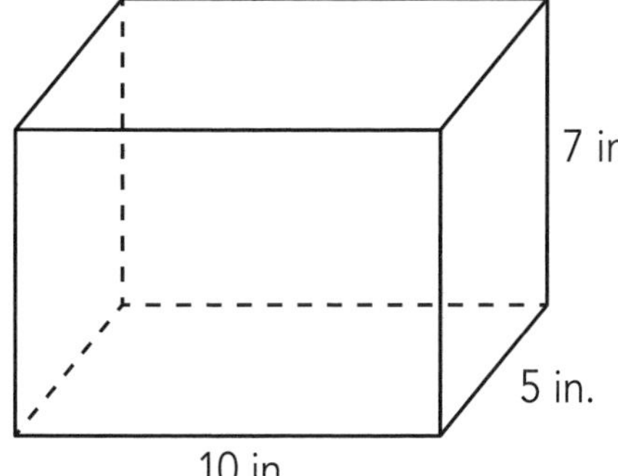

1. SA = ______________________

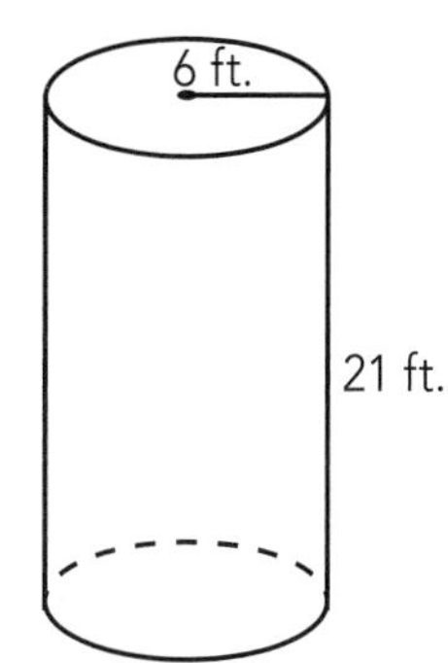

2. SA = ______________________

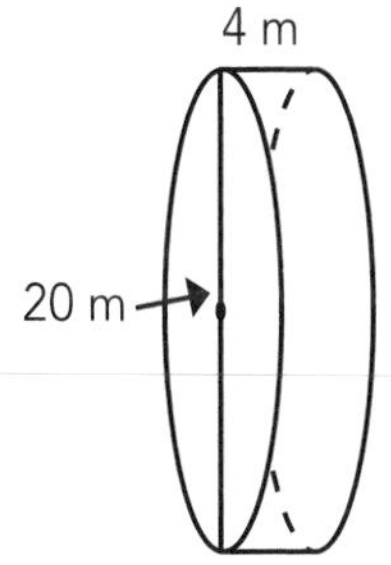

3. SA = ______________________

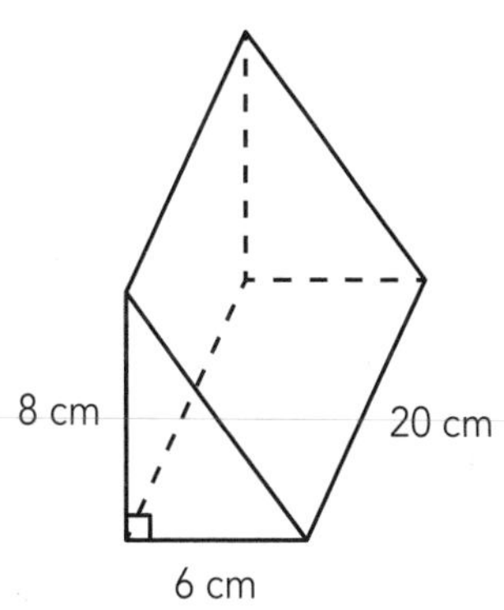

4. SA = ______________________

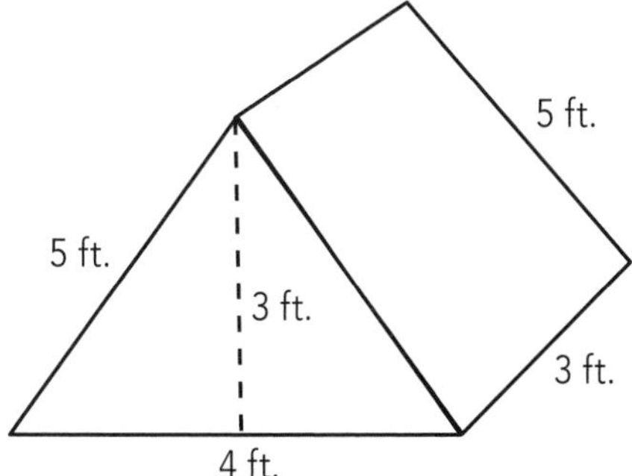

5. SA = ______________________

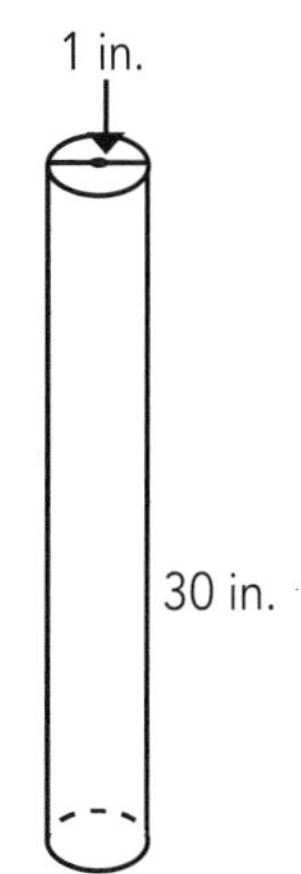

6. SA = ______________________

Volume Practice

Find the volume of each solid. Use $\pi = 3.14$ when necessary. Round your answers to the nearest hundredth.

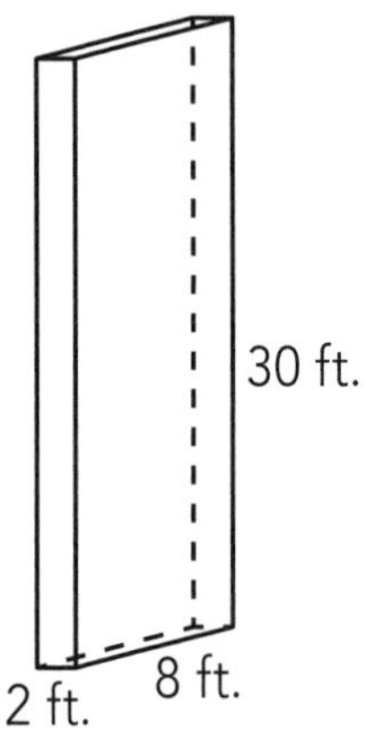

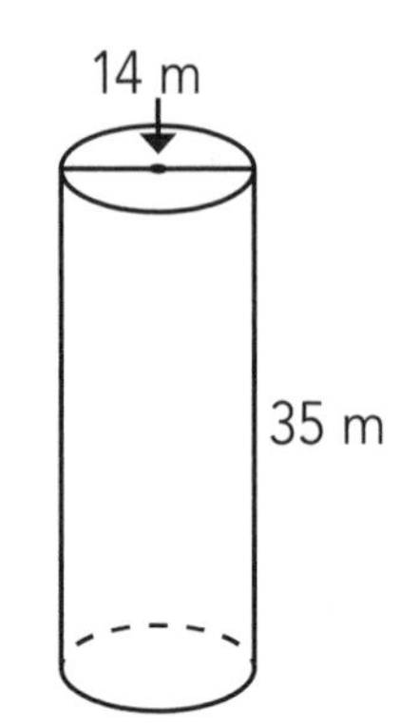

1. V = ____________________

2. V = ____________________

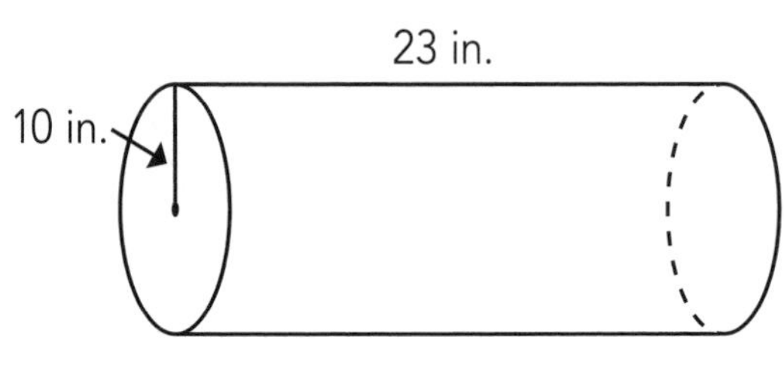

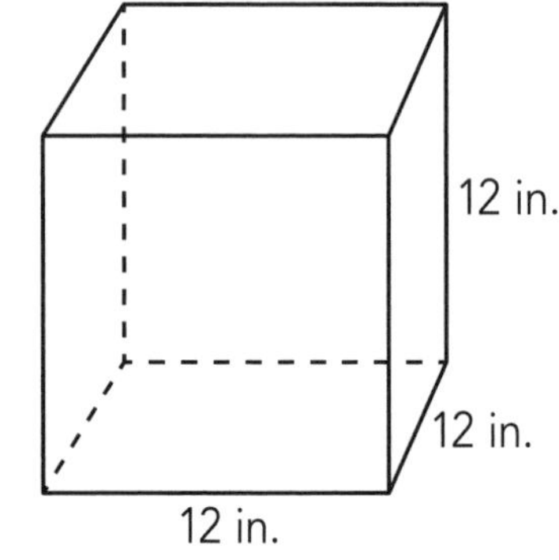

3. V = ____________________

4. V = ____________________

5. The inside dimensions of a microwave oven are 9" x 12" x 18". (1 cubic foot = 12" x 12" x 12"). What is its volume in cubic feet?

____

6. The inside dimensions of a chest freezer are 24" x 24" x 36". What is its volume in cubic feet?

____

Volume of a Sphere

Solids

To find the volume of a sphere, use the following formula:

$$V = \frac{4}{3}\pi r^3$$

$$V = \frac{4}{3}(3.14)(3^3)$$

$$V = 113.04$$

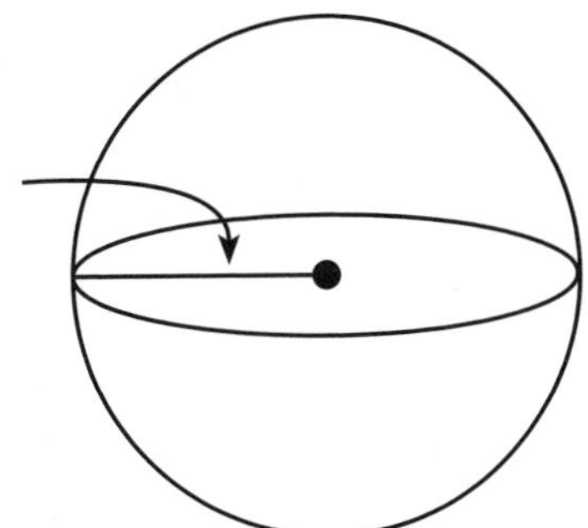

Find the volume of each sphere with the given radius or diameter. Use $\pi = 3.14$. Round your answers to the nearest hundredth.

1. r = 5 in.

V = ____________

2. d = 14 ft.

V = ____________

3. d = 24 mi.

V = ____________

4. r = 10 cm

V= ____________

Identifying Transformations

The **image** of an object is the figure formed after the object has been transformed. There are four major types of transformations.

- **Translation**—An object is translated when it is moved in any direction.

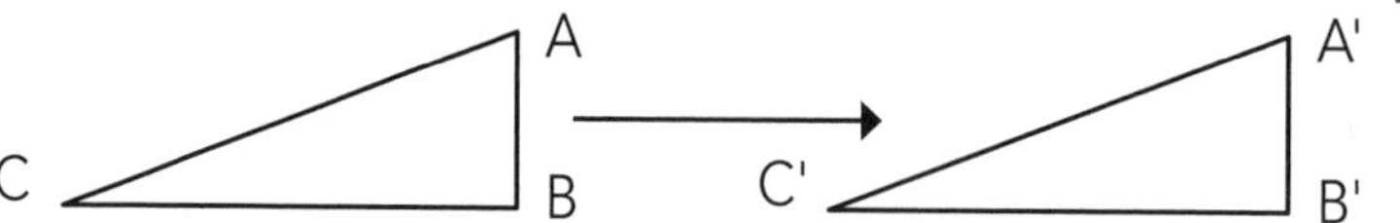

- **Reflection**—An object is reflected when it is flipped over a line of symmetry.
- **Rotation**—An object is rotated when it is turned around a center point.

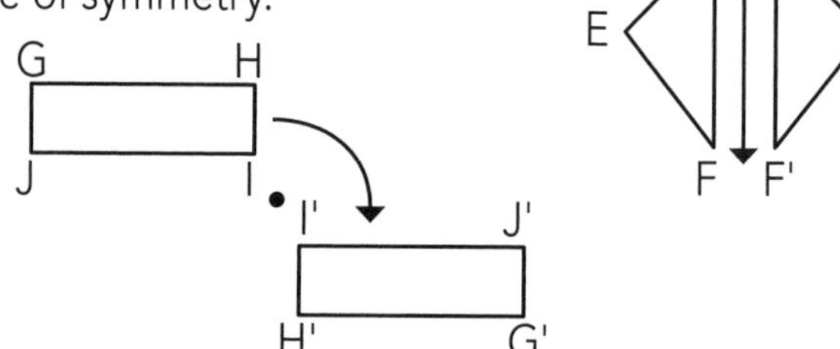

- **Dilation**—An object is dilated when it is enlarged or reduced with respect to a point of dilation.

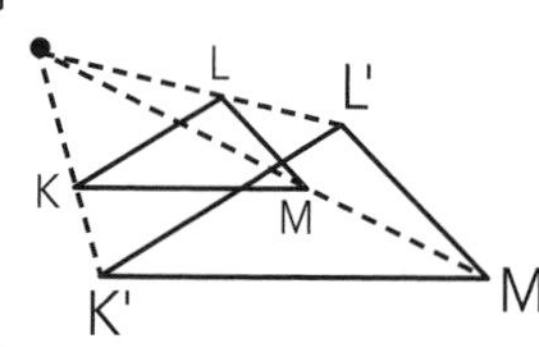

Name the type of transformation that created each image.

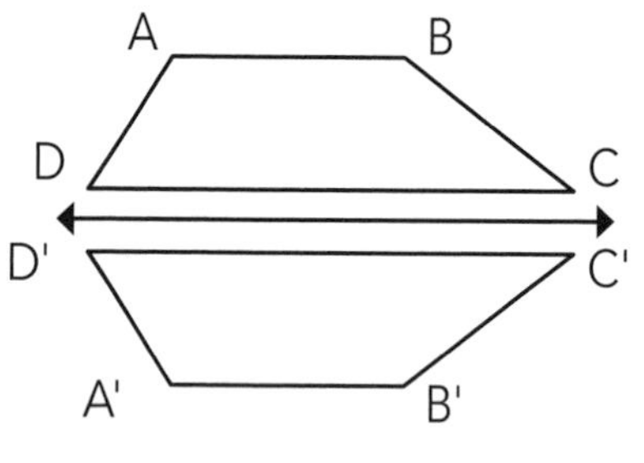

1. ______________________

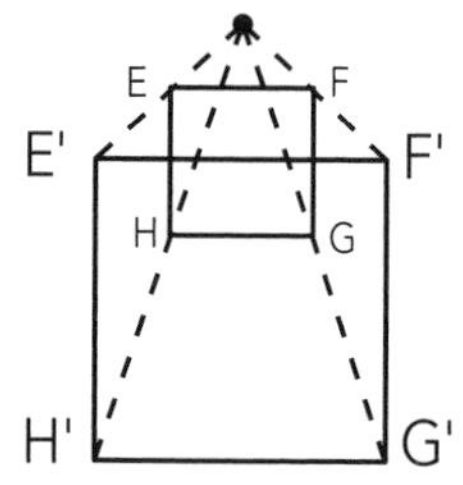

2. ______________________

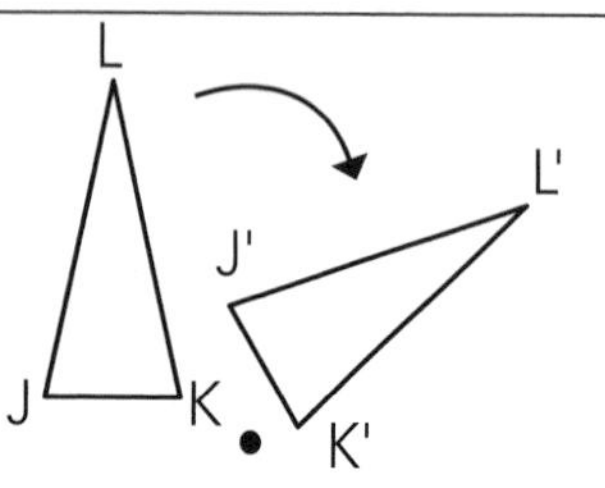

3. ______________________

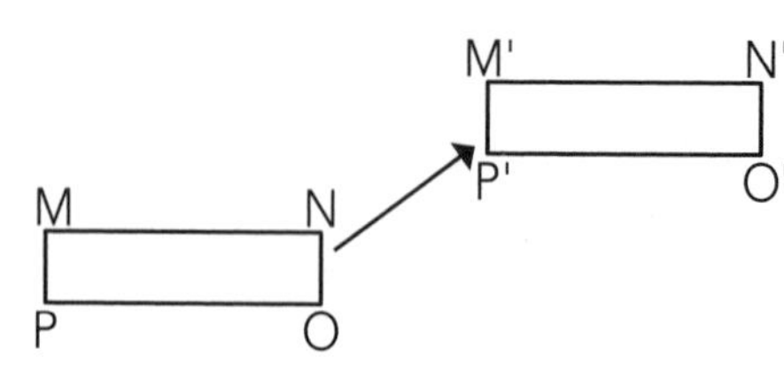

4. ______________________

Drawing Transformations

Transformations

Draw the image that would be created after the given transformation.

1. reflection

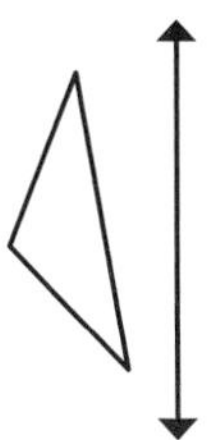

2. 180° rotation about point P

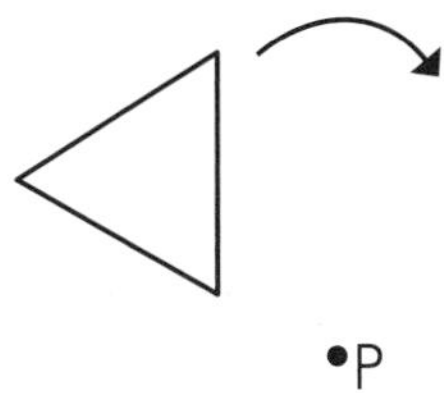

3. dilation from point P

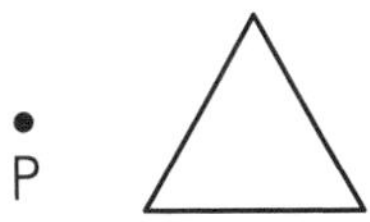

4. translation to the right

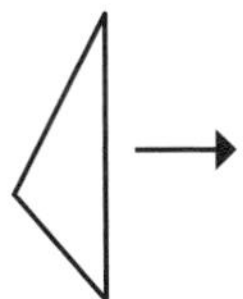

5. 90° rotation about point P

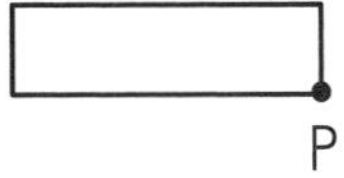

6. translation down

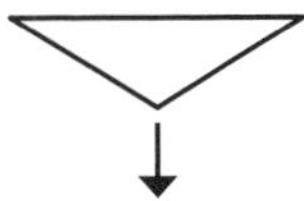

7. reflection

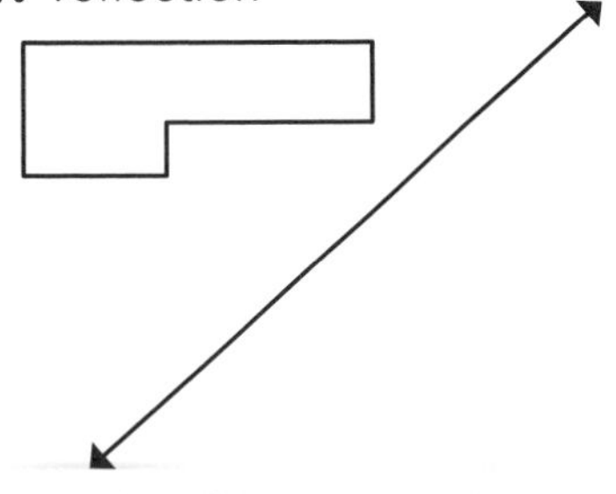

8. dilation from point P

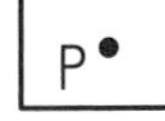

Symmetry

When you draw a line through the center of a figure, and the two resulting figures are reflections of each other, then the figure has **reflectional symmetry**. A figure can have vertical reflectional symmetry, horizontal reflectional symmetry, or both.

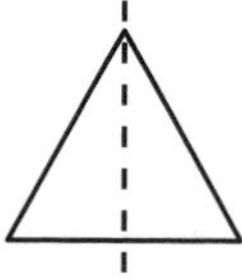

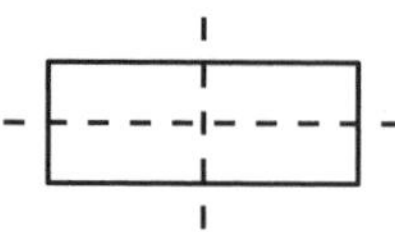

When you rotate a figure about a central point, and the resulting image is congruent to the original figure, then the figure has **rotational symmetry**.

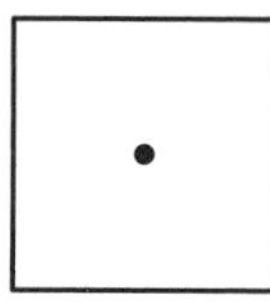

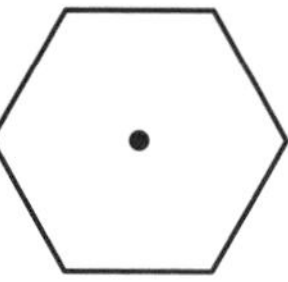

Determine whether each figure has reflectional symmetry, rotational symmetry, or neither.

1. ______________________

2. ______________________

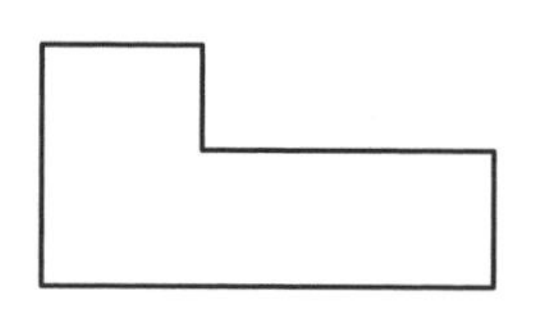

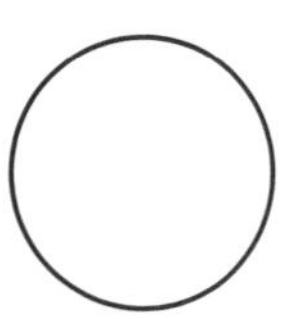

3. ______________________

4. ______________________

Look at the uppercase English alphabet below. Which letters have:

A B C D E F G H I J K L M N O P Q R S T U V W X Y Z

5. reflectional symmetry

____

6. rotational symmetry

____

7. both types of symmetry

____

8. neither type of symmetry

____

Identifying Points in a Coordinate Plane

Coordinate Geometry

Each point in a coordinate plane is a result of two transformations: a horizontal translation (*x*-coordinate) and a vertical translation (*y*-coordinate).

To describe the location of a point, use an ordered pair (*x*, *y*).

A (1, 2)
right 1, up 2

B (−2, −1)
left 2, down 1

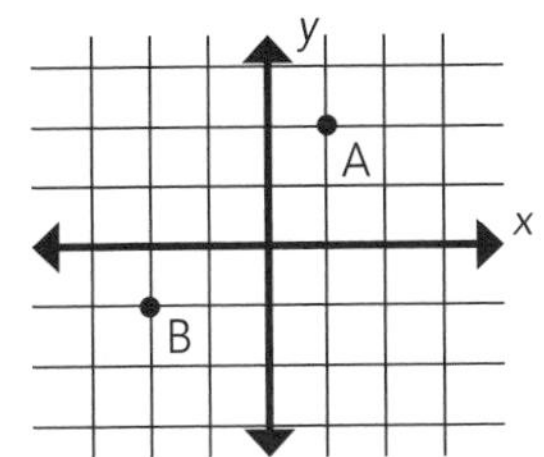

Give the ordered pair for each point on the graph.

1. A ________

2. B ________

3. C ________

4. D ________

5. E ________

6. F ________

7. G ________

8. H ________

9. I ________

10. J ________

11. K ________

12. L ________

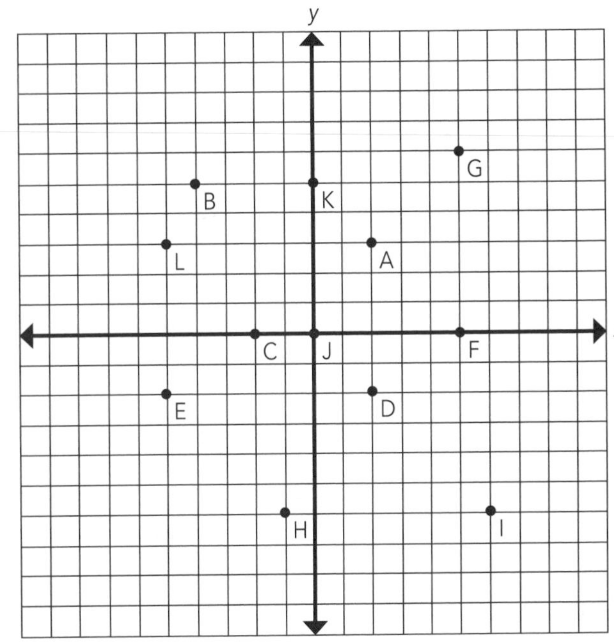

Plotting Points in a Coordinate Plane

Coordinate Geometry

Plot and label these ordered pairs as points on the coordinate plane.

1. A (−3, 4)
2. B (2, 0)
3. C (0, −3)
4. D (1, 4)
5. E (−3, −1)
6. F (2, 2)
7. G (2, −2)
8. H (−1, −2)

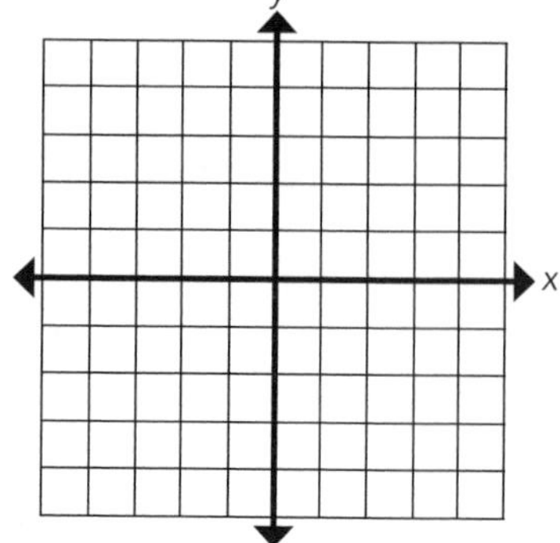

Plot these ordered pairs in order as points on the coordinate plane. Connect the points with segments as you make them. Do not connect points with the word *break* between them. The result will spell a message.

A (−6, 3)
B (−6, 6)
C (−5, 5)
D (−4, 6)
E (−4, 3)
break
F (−3, 3)
G (−2, 6)
H (−1, 3)
break
I (−2.5, 4)
J (−1.5, 4)
break
K (0, 6)

L (2, 6)
M (1, 6)
N (1, 3)
break
O (3, 6)
P (3, 3)
Q (3, 4.5)
R (5, 4.5)
S (5, 3)
T (5, 6)
break
U (−3, 2)
V (−1, 2)
W (−2, 2)

X (−2, −1)
Y (−3, −1)
Z (−1, −1)
break
AA (2, 2)
BB (0, 2)
CC (0, 1)
DD (2, 1)
EE (2, −1)
FF (0, −1)
break
GG (−2, −2)
HH (−4, −2)
II (−4, −5)

JJ (−4, −3.5)
KK (−3, −3.5)
break
LL (−1, −2)
MM (−1, −5)
NN (1, −5)

OO (1, −2)
break
PP (2, −5)
QQ (2, −2)
RR (4, −5)
SS (4, −2)

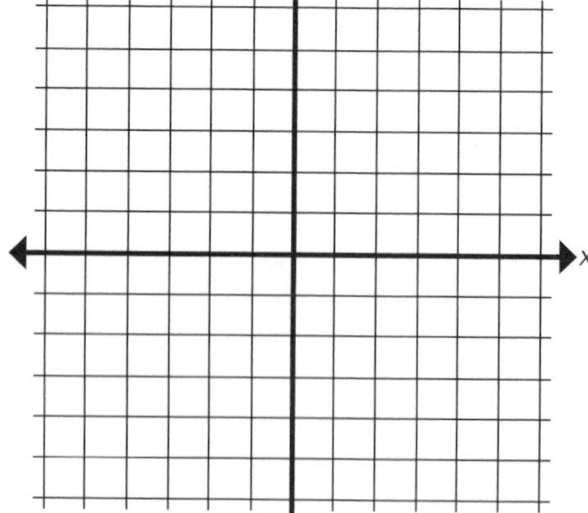

Coordinate Translations

Coordinate Geometry

Each point of ΔABC has been translated left 3 units and up 4 units. The image figure is labeled $\Delta A'B'C'$.

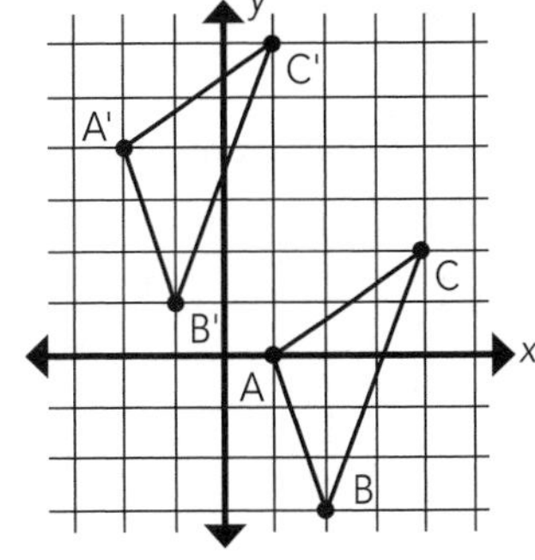

A (1, 0) → A' (1 – 3, 0 + 4) = A' (⁻2, 4)
B (2, ⁻3) → B' (2 – 3, ⁻3 + 4) = B' (⁻1, 1)
C (4, 2) → C' (4 – 3, 2 + 4) = C' (1, 6)

1. Translate ΔGHI to the left 1 unit and up 3 units. Give the coordinates of the image points.

G' (_____ , _____)

H' (_____ , _____)

I' (_____ , _____)

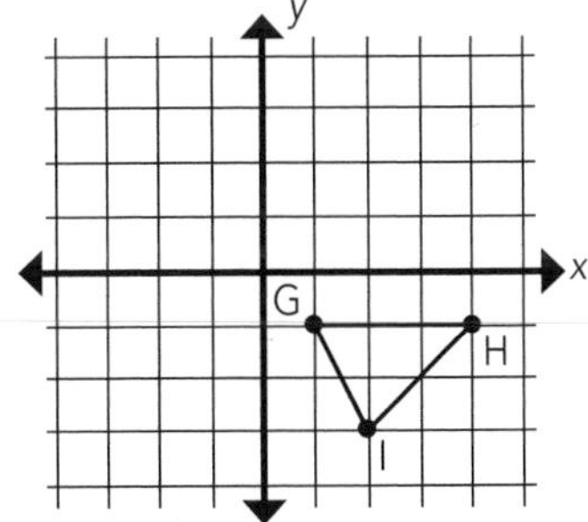

2. Translate rectangle WXYZ to the left 3 units. Give the coordinates of the image points.

W' (_____ , _____)

X' (_____ , _____)

Y' (_____ , _____)

Z' (_____ , _____)

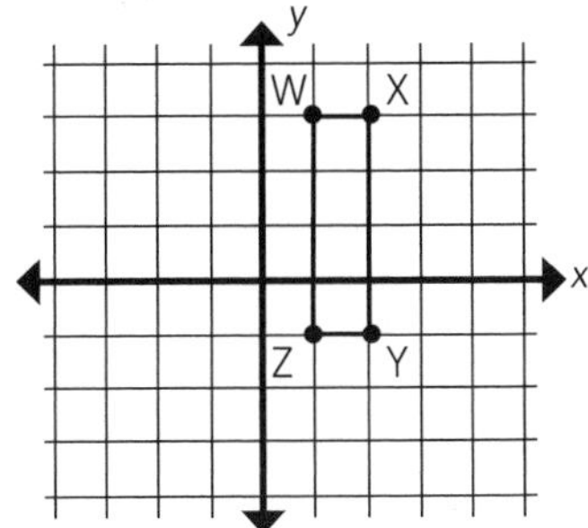

Coordinate Reflections

Coordinate Geometry

Each point of ΔABC has been reflected over the *x*-axis.
The image figure is labeled ΔA'B'C'.

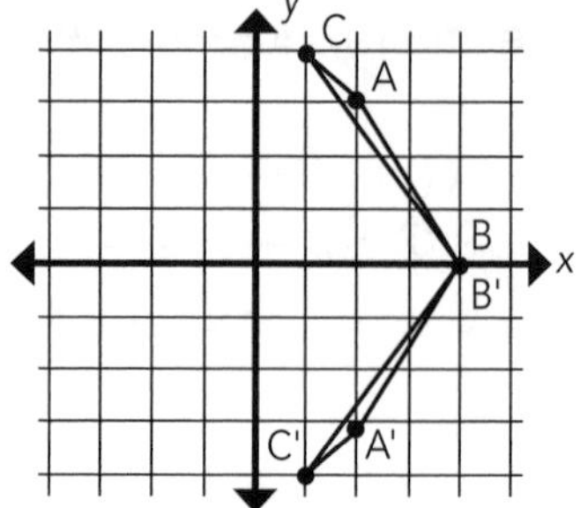

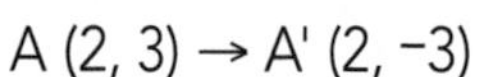

A (2, 3) → A' (2, −3)
B (4, 0) → B' (4, 0)
C (1, 4) → C' (1, −4)

1. Reflect $\overline{AB}$ over the *y*-axis.
Give the coordinates of the image points.

A' (_____ , _____)

B' (_____ , _____)

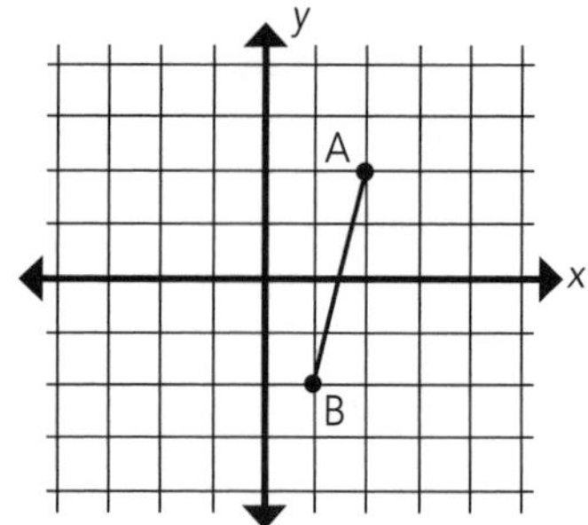

2. Reflect rectangle WXYZ over the *x*-axis.
Give the coordinates of the image points.

W' (_____ , _____)

X' (_____ , _____)

Y' (_____ , _____)

Z' (_____ , _____)

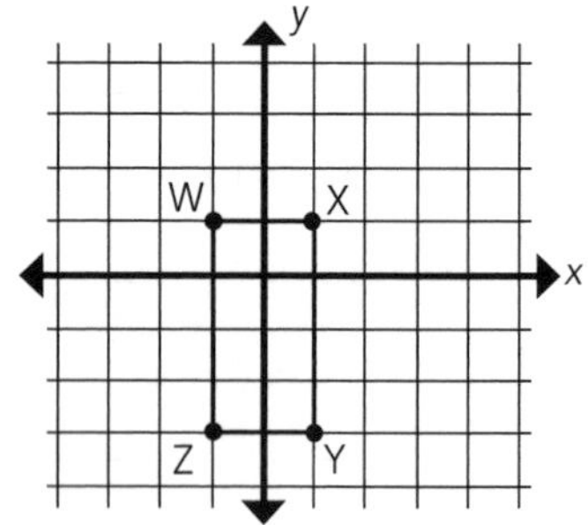

Coordinate Rotations

Coordinate Geometry

Each point of ΔABC has been rotated 90° clockwise around the **origin** (0, 0). The image figure is labeled ΔA'B'C'.

A (−3, 1) → A' (1, 3)
B (−2, 4) → B' (4, 2)
C (−1, 1) → C' (1, 1)

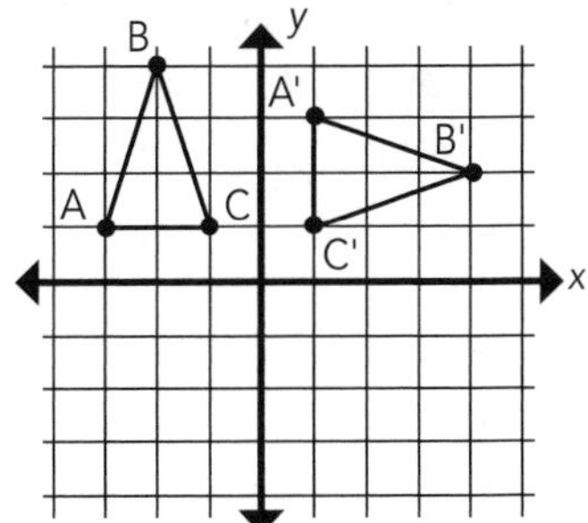

1. Rotate $\overline{AB}$ 180° clockwise around the origin. Give the coordinates of the image points.

A' (_____ , _____)

B' (_____ , _____)

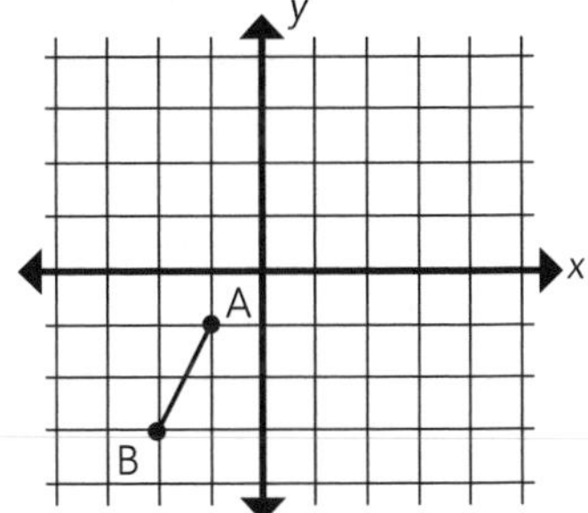

2. Rotate ΔDEF 90° clockwise around the origin. Give the coordinates of the image points.

D' (_____ , _____)

E' (_____ , _____)

F' (_____ , _____)

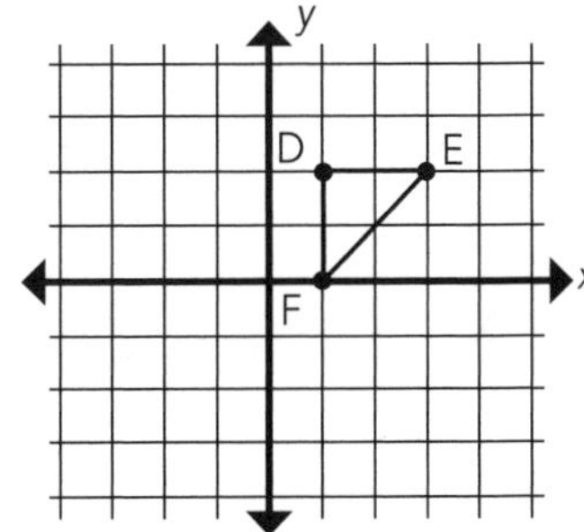

Coordinate Dilations

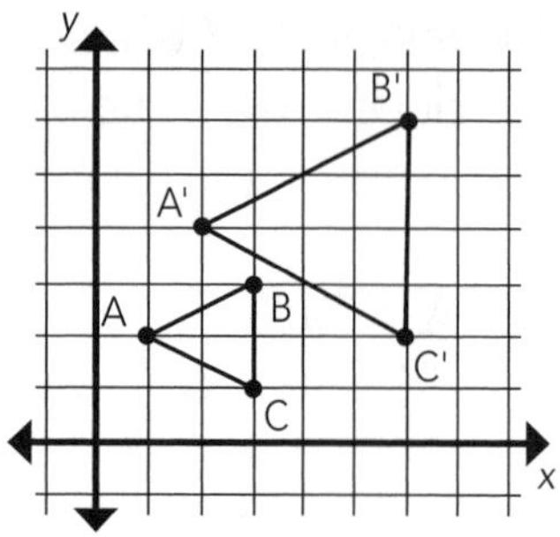

Each point of ΔABC has been dilated from the origin. The image is twice as large as the original figure. The image figure is labeled ΔA'B'C'.

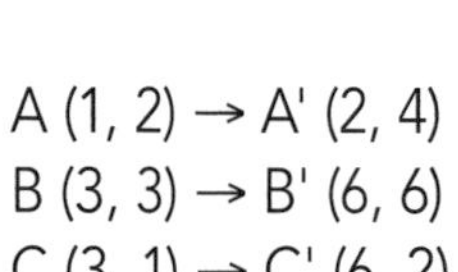
A (1, 2) → A' (2, 4)
B (3, 3) → B' (6, 6)
C (3, 1) → C' (6, 2)

1. Dilate $\overline{AB}$ from the origin. Make the image three times as large as the original. Give the coordinates of the image points.

A' (_____ , _____)

B' (_____ , _____)

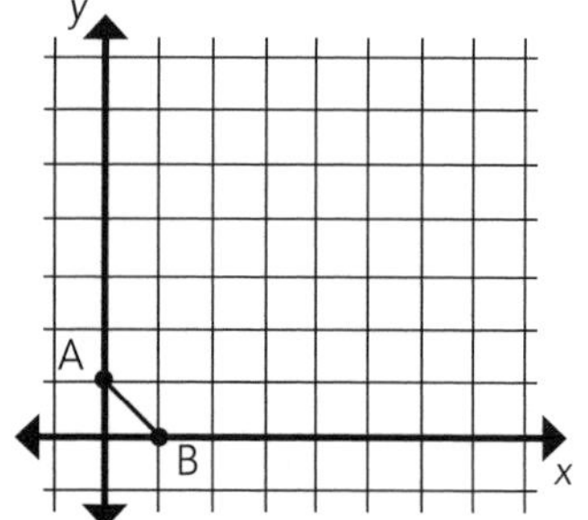

2. Dilate WXYZ from the origin. Make the image twice as large as the original. Give the coordinates of the image points.

W' (_____ , _____)

X' (_____ , _____)

Y' (_____ , _____)

Z' (_____ , _____)

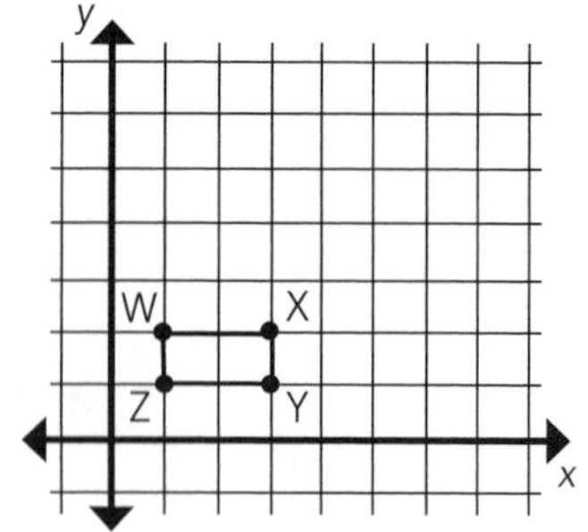

The Midpoint Formula

Coordinate Geometry

The midpoint of a segment whose endpoints have coordinates (x_1, y_1) and (x_2, y_2) will have coordinates $\left(\frac{x_1 + y_2}{2}, \frac{x_1 + y_2}{2}\right)$

Midpoint $\left(\frac{-2 + 3}{2}, \frac{4 + -2}{2}\right) = \left(\frac{1}{2}, 1\right)$

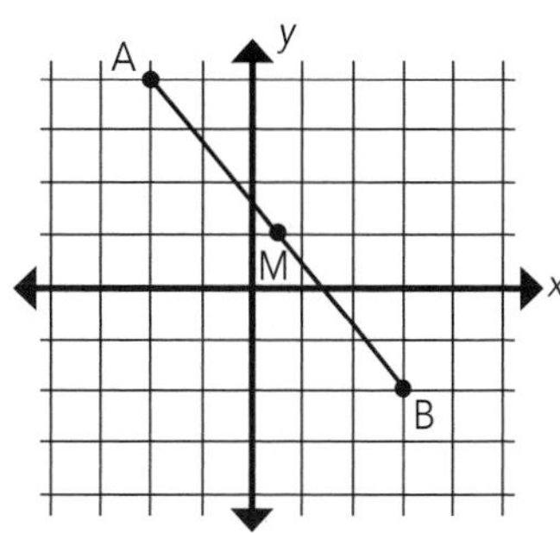

Given the coordinates for endpoints A and B, find the coordinates of the midpoint of $\overline{AB}$. Use the coordinate plane to draw each segment $\overline{AB}$ and its midpoint.

1. A(3, 5) B(−2, 1) M(___,___)

2. A(0, 0) B(4, −7) M(___,___)

3. A(−1, 4) B(−8, 4) M(___,___)

4. A(5, −2) B(−3, 1) M(___,___)

5. A(7, 3) B(−2, 0) M(___,___)

6. A(−1, 2) B(6, 6) M(___,___)

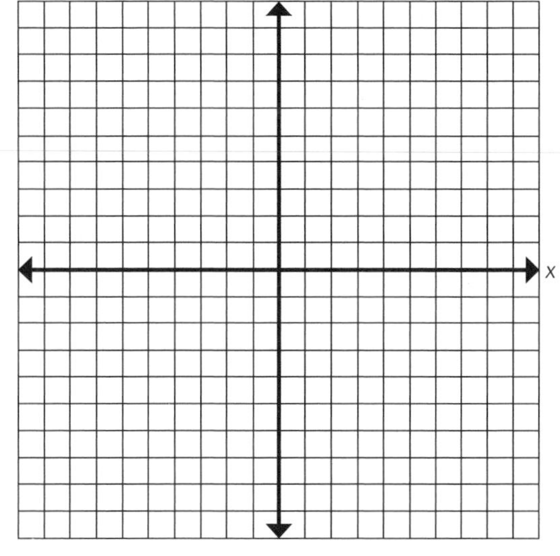

Given the coordinates for endpoint A and midpoint M, find the coordinates of endpoint B for each segment $\overline{AB}$.

7. A(3, 2) M(4, 4) B(___,___)

8. A(−2, −5) M(2, 0) B(___,___)

The Distance Formula

Coordinate Geometry

The length of a segment whose endpoints have coordinates (x_1, y_1) and (x_2, y_2) can be found using the formula $d = \sqrt{(x_2 - x_1)^2 + (y_2 - y_1)^2}$

$d = \sqrt{(x_2 - x_1)^2 + (y_2 - y_1)^2}$

$d = \sqrt{(3 - (-2))^2 + (-2 - 4)^2}$

$d = \sqrt{5^2 + (-6)^2}$

$d = \sqrt{25 + 36}$

$d = \sqrt{61}$

$\overline{AB} \approx 7.81$

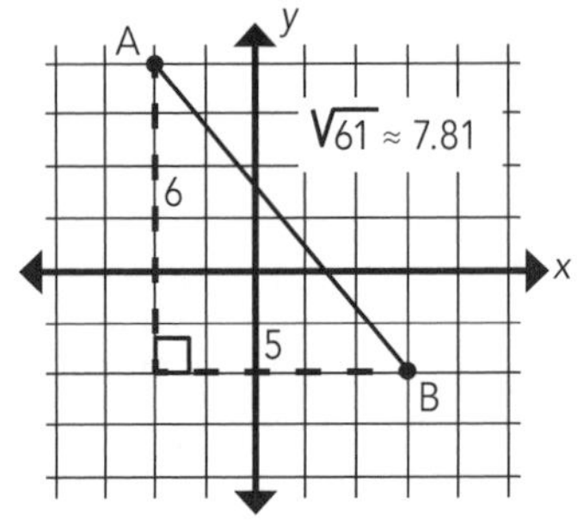

Given the coordinates for endpoints *A* and *B*, find the length of $\overline{AB}$. Round your answers to the nearest hundredth.

1. A(3, 3) B(−2, 1) $\overline{AB}$ = ______

2. A(0, 0) B(4, −6) $\overline{AB}$ = ______

3. A(2, 4) B(−7, 4) $\overline{AB}$ = ______

4. A(5, −2) B(−2, 1) $\overline{AB}$ = ______

5. A(7, 3) B(0, 4) $\overline{AB}$ = ______

6. A(−1, 2) B(6, 6) $\overline{AB}$ = ______

Answer Key

PAGES 4–6—ASSESSMENT TEST

1. 15 m^3, 46 m
2. 25, 38
3. line, segment, ray
4. 24, 24
5. 9, 20, 40
6. 10048 mm^3, 2637.6 mm^2
7. A' = (2, 2), B' = (1, -1)
8. 80 ft.
9. 65°, acute; 40°, acute; 120°, obtuse
10. 43.96 cm., 615.44 cm^2
11. 114°, 114°
12. 90°, 50°, 56°
13. D' = (-2, -1), E' = (0, -3), F' = (3, -1)
14. 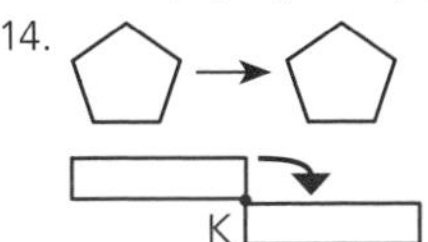

15. 720°, 1080°

PAGE 8—ALONG THE LINES

1. line, $\overleftrightarrow{MN}$ or $\overleftrightarrow{NM}$
2. segment, $\overline{OP}$ or $\overline{PO}$
3. ray, $\overrightarrow{RQ}$
4. plane STU
5. ray, $\overrightarrow{WX}$ or $\overrightarrow{WV}$
6. segment $\overline{YZ}$ or $\overline{ZY}$
7. •A •C •B
8. H I
9. X Y
10. S T

PAGE 9—LINEAR RELATIONSHIPS

1. $\overleftrightarrow{BF} \parallel \overleftrightarrow{GC}$
2. $\overleftrightarrow{EH}$ and $\overleftrightarrow{BF}$ or $\overleftrightarrow{GC}$
3. $\overleftrightarrow{AG} \perp \overleftrightarrow{BF}$ or $\overleftrightarrow{AG} \perp \overleftrightarrow{GC}$
4. B, D, F; E, F, G, H; A, D, G
5. any three points not on the same line
6. yes

PAGE 10—CONGRUENT SEGMENTS AND SEGMENT ADDITION

1. 2 2. 4 3. 9 4. 4 5. 13
6. 17 7. $\overline{DF}$ 8. $\overline{AC}$ 9. $\overline{BC}$ or $\overline{DE}$

PAGE 11—MIDPOINTS

1. point D 2. 2 3. E 4. 5
5. E 6. $\overline{IK}$ 7. 10 8. F
9. D or J 10. x = 15 11. 50 12. 100

PAGE 12—NAMING, MEASURING, AND CLASSIFYING ANGLES

1. 20°, acute 2. 90°, right 3. 160°, obtuse

PAGE 12—CONTINUED

4. 113°, obtuse 5. 70°, acute 6. 159°, obtuse
7. 63°, acute 8. 90°, right 9. 140°, obtuse

PAGE 13—CONGRUENT ANGLES AND ANGLE ADDITION

1. 60° 2. 70° 3. 145° 4. 180°
5. ∠DKG or ∠BKE 6. ∠CKE 7. ∠BKD
8. 100° 9. 105° 10. 90°

PAGE 14—ANGLE BISECTORS

1. 45° 2. ∠CBD 3. ∠MNO 4. 32°
5. 64° 6. ∠YXZ 7. 67° 8. 67°
9. $\overrightarrow{NO}$ 10. $\overrightarrow{XY}$

PAGE 15—COMPLEMENTARY AND SUPPLEMENTARY ANGLES

1. ∠ABC 2. 120° 3. 22° 4. ∠GFH 5. 29°
6. ∠ONP 7. 45° 8. 63° 9. 135° 10. 160°

PAGE 16—VERTICAL ANGLES

1. ∠7 2. ∠8 3. 31°
4. 149° 5. 149° 6. 130°
7. 50° 8. 50° 9. 360°

PAGE 17—CORRESPONDING ANGLES

1. x = 120° 2. x = 117° 3. x = 6 4. x = 126°

PAGE 18—ALTERNATE INTERIOR AND EXTERIOR ANGLES

1. x = 108° 2. x = 109° 3. x = 5 4. x = 10

PAGE 19—SAME-SIDE INTERIOR ANGLES

1. x = 75° 2.x = 0 3. x = 45°
4. All angles are either 60° or 120°.

PAGE 20—CLASSIFYING POLYGONS

1. B, D 2. heptagon 3. pentagon
4. quadrilateral 5. hexagon

PAGE 21—POLYGON ANGLE MEASURES

1. 720° 2. 360° 3. 1,080° 4. 900°
5. 540° 6. 180° 7. x = 75° 8. x = 117°
9. x = 150° 10. x = 75°

PAGE 22—REGULAR AND IRREGULAR POLYGONS

1. regular 2. irregular 3. irregular 4. regular
5. 60° 6. 90° 7. 108° 8. 120°
9. 128.57° 10. 135°

PAGE 23—DRAWING POLYGONS

Answers will vary.

PAGE 24—CONGRUENT POLYGONS

1. ∠V 2. $\overline{YX}$ 3. 105° 4. $\overline{VW}$
5. 6 6. 83° 7. 80° 8. 5

Answer Key

Page 25—Classifying Triangles

1. acute, equilateral
2. obtuse, scalene
3. acute, scalene
4. right, isosceles
5. acute, scalene
6. obtuse, isosceles
7. no
8. no
9. yes

Page 26—Triangle Sum Theorem

1. 51°
2. 72°
3. 103°
4. 50°
5. 18°
6. x = 35°

Page 27—Angle Measures of Triangles

1. x = 70°, y = 40°
2. x = 60°, y = 60°
3. x = 50°, z = 56°
4. x = 11°, y = 11°
5. x = 91°, y = 63°, z = 26°
6. x = 45°, y = 45°

Page 28—Angle Puzzle

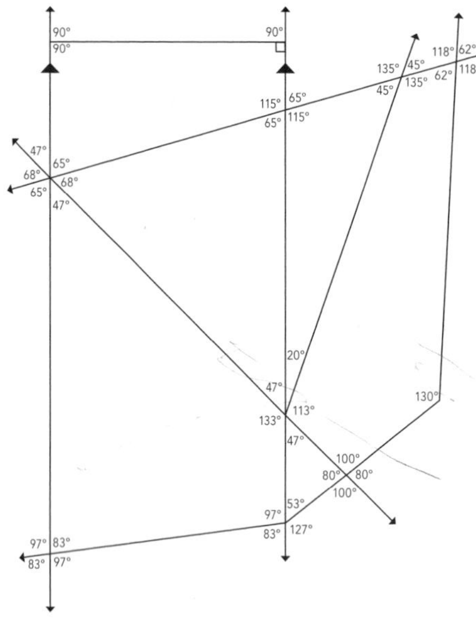

Page 29—Congruent Triangles

1. yes, SAS
2. no
3. no
4. yes, SSS
5. yes, SAS or SSS
6. yes, SAS

Page 30—Congruent Triangles, cont.

1. yes, ASA
2. no
3. yes, SAS
4. yes, HL
5. yes, AAS
6. no

Page 31—Parts of Congruent Triangles

1. 8 ($\overline{DC}$)
2. 30°
3. 60°
4. 10 ($\overline{GI}$)
5. 5 ($\overline{UV}$)
6. 57°

Page 32—The Pythagorean Theorem

1. $c = 13$
2. $a = 7$
3. $c = 4.24$
4. $a = 28.28$
5. $b = 20$
6. $c = 17.89$

Page 33—Applying the Pythagorean Theorem

1. 13.60 cm
2. 7.07 m
3. 7.07 ft.
4. 41.23 ft.
5. 0.90 miles

Page 34—The Converse of the Pythagorean Theorem

1. right
2. acute
3. obtuse
4. right
5. right
6. obtuse
7. obtuse
8. acute
9. right
10. right

Page 35—Classifying Quadrilaterals

1. parallelogram
2. trapezoid
3. square
4. rectangle
5. trapezoid
6. rhombus

Page 36—Angle Measures of Quadrilaterals

1. m∠A = 64°, m∠B = 116°, m∠D = 116°
2. m∠W = 50°, m∠Y = 90°
3. m∠N = 61°
4. m∠V = 90°
5. m∠F = 55°, m∠G = 55°, m∠D = 125°

Page 37—Side Lengths of Quadrilaterals

1. BC = 6, CD = 8
2. WX = WZ = YZ = 10
3. NO = 7
4. PQ = 13
5. m∠I = 64°, m∠J = 116°, m∠H = 116°

Page 38—Solving Proportions

1. $x = 3$
2. $x = 15$
3. $x = 10.5$
4. $x = \frac{130}{3} = 43\frac{1}{3}$
5. $x = 132$
6. $x = 21$

Page 39—Similar Polygons

1. no
2. yes
3. yes
4. yes
5. yes

Page 40—Similar Triangles

1. yes, AA~
2. no
3. yes, SAS~
4. no
5. yes, SAS~
6. yes, AA~

Page 41—Applying Similarity

1. 99°
2. 112°
3. 92°
4. 125°
5. 7
6. 8
7. 4
8. 2.5

Page 42—Applying Similarity, cont.

1. 937.5 miles
2. 270,000 sq. km
3. 12.5 cm
4. 100 ft.

Page 43—Solving Perimeter Problems

1. 21
2. 52
3. 48
4. 54
5. 42
6. 40

Answer Key

PAGE 44—AREA OF QUADRILATERALS
1. 100 cm^2 2. 60 $ft.^2$ 3. 36
4. 28 cm^2 5. 0.5 6. 12

PAGE 45—AREA OF TRIANGLES AND TRAPEZOIDS
1. 58.5 $in.^2$ 2. 90 3. 14 $in.^2$
4. 52.5 5. 42

PAGE 46—AREA OF IRREGULAR SHAPES
1. 63 2. 276 3. 90 4. 76

PAGE 47—AREA OF A SHADED REGION
1. 18 2. 37 3. 77.5
4. 92 5. 225 6. 31

PAGE 48—PROPORTIONAL PERIMETER AND AREA
1. Perimeter: 16, 32, 48 Area: 15, 60, 135
2. Perimeter: 4, 8, 12 Area: 1, 4, 9
3. 2, 4
4. 3, 9

PAGE 49—PARTS OF CIRCLES
1. $\overline{AE}$, $\overline{BC}$, $\overline{EC}$, $\overline{DB}$, $\overline{EA}$, $\overline{CB}$, $\overline{CE}$, $\overline{BD}$
2. $\overline{EC}$, $\overline{DB}$, $\overline{CE}$, $\overline{BD}$
3. $\overline{XE}$, $\overline{XD}$, $\overline{XB}$, $\overline{XC}$, $\overline{EX}$, $\overline{DX}$, $\overline{BX}$, $\overline{CX}$
4. diameter, chord
5. radius
6. none of these
7. radius
8. chord
9. none of these

PAGE 50—DISCOVERING PI
Answers will vary, however every entry in the $C \div d$ column should be approximately equal to 3.14.

PAGE 51—CIRCUMFERENCE
1. 72.22 in. 2. 62.8 m 3. 50.24 cm
4. 53.38 cm 5. 10 in. 6. 14 cm

PAGE 52—AREA OF CIRCLES
1. 314 m^2 2. 153.86 $ft.^2$ 3. 12.56 $ft.^2$
4. 346.19 $in.^2$ 5. 72.35 cm^2 6. 78.5 cm^2

PAGE 53—CLASSIFYING SOLIDS
1. triangular pyramid 2. cone
3. cylinder 4. hexagonal prism

PAGE 54—DRAWING SOLIDS
Answers will vary.

PAGE 55—PARTS OF A PRISM
1. 6, 9, 5 2. 10, 15, 7
3. 12, 18, 8 4. 14, 21, 9

PAGE 55—CONTINUED
5. 16, 24, 10 6. 2x, 3x, x + 2

PAGE 56—VIEWING SOLIDS FROM DIFFERENT PERSPECTIVES

1. Front: 
2. Front: 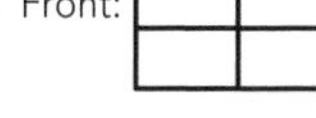

Side: 

Side:

Top: 

Top:

PAGE 57—VIEWING SOLIDS FROM DIFFERENT PERSPECTIVES, CONT.

1. 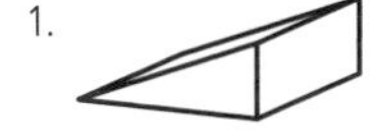

2.

PAGE 58—NETS

1.

2.

3.

4.

5. octagonal prism 6. triangular pyramid

PAGE 59—SURFACE AREA OF A PRISM
1. 208 $in.^2$ 2. 132 cm^2
3. 384 $ft.^2$ 4. 1,350 $yd.^2$

PAGE 60—VOLUME OF A PRISM
1. 120 cm^3 2. 60 m^3 3. 60 $ft.^3$
4. 1,000 $ft.^3$ 5. 72 $ft.^3$

PAGE 61—SURFACE AREA OF A CYLINDER
1. 678.24 cm^2 2. 753.6 mm^2 3. 427.04 $in.^2$
4. 1,168.08 mm^2 5. 1,570 $ft.^2$ 6. 427.04 cm^2

PAGE 62—VOLUME OF A CYLINDER
1. 9,734 mm^3 2. 706.5 $ft.^3$ 3. 904.32 $in.^3$
4. 40.82 $in.^3$ 5. 1,177.5 $in.^3$ 6. 1,134.325 m^3

PAGE 63—SURFACE AREA PRACTICE
1. 310 $in.^2$ 2. 1,017.36 $ft.^2$ 3. 879.2 m^2
4. 528 cm^2 5. 54 $ft.^2$ 6. 95.77 $in.^2$

Answer Key

PAGE 64—VOLUME PRACTICE

1. 480 ft.^{3} 2. 5,385.1 m^3 3. 7,222 in.^{3}
4. 1,728 in.^{3} 5. 1.125 cu. ft.^{3} 6. 12 cu. ft.^{3}

PAGE 65—VOLUME OF A SPHERE

1. 523.33 in.^{3} 2. 1,436.03 ft.^{3}
3. 7,234.56 mi.^{3} 4. 4,186.67 cm^3

PAGE 66—IDENTIFYING TRANSFORMATIONS

1. reflection 2. dilation
3. rotation 4. translation

PAGE 67—DRAWING TRANSFORMATIONS

1.

2.

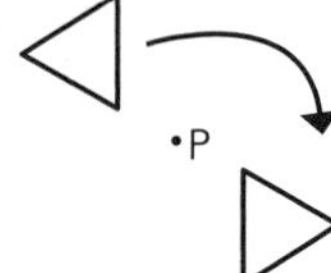

3.

4.

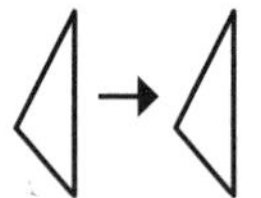

5.

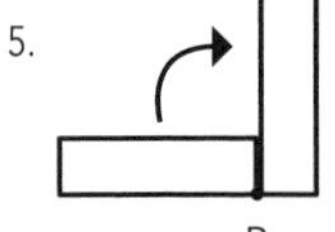

6.

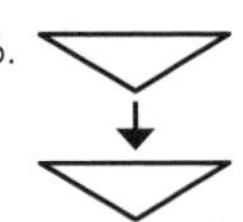

7.

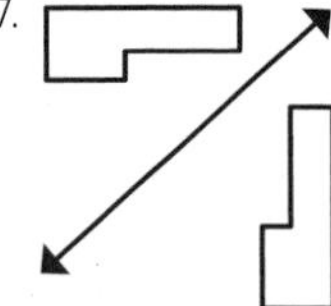

8. P

PAGE 68—SYMMETRY

1. reflection
2. reflection and rotation
3. neither
4. reflection and rotation
5. A, B, C, D, E, H, I, K, M, O, T, U, V, W, X, Y
6. H, I, N, O, S, X, Z
7. H, I, O, X
8. F, G, J, L, P, Q, R

PAGE 69—IDENTIFYING POINTS IN A COORDINATE PLANE

1. (2, 3) 2. (−4, 5)
3. (−2, 0) 4. (2, −2)
5. (−5, −2) 6. (5, 0)
7. (5, 6) 8. (−1, −6)
9. (6, −6) 10. (0, 0)
11. (0, 5) 12. (−5, 3)

PAGE 70—PLOTTING POINTS IN A COORDINATE PLANE

1. through 8.

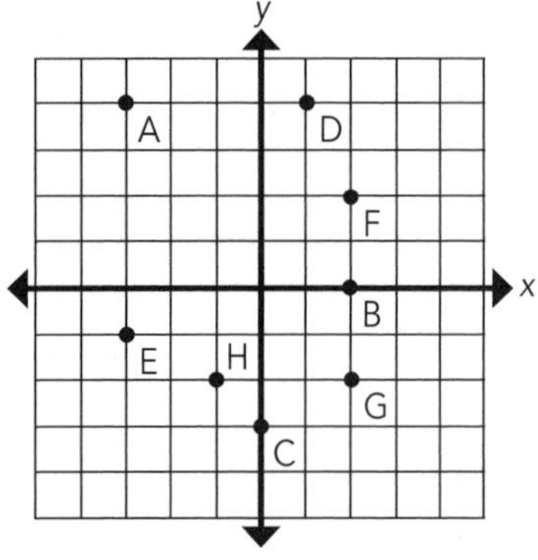

Message: MATH IS FUN

PAGE 71—COORDINATE TRANSLATIONS

1. G'(0, 2), H'(3, 2), I'(1, 0)
2. W'(−2, 3), X'(−1, 3), Y'(−1, −1), Z'(−2, −1)

PAGE 72—COORDINATE REFLECTIONS

1. A'(−2, 2), B'(−1, −2)
2. W'(−1, −1), X'(1, −1), Y'(1, 3), Z'(−1, 3)

PAGE 73—COORDINATE ROTATIONS

1. A'(1, 1), B'(2, 3)
2. D'(2, −1), E'(2, −3), F'(0, −1)

PAGE 74—COORDINATE DILATIONS

1. A'(0, 3), B'(3, 0)
2. W'(2, 4), X'(6, 4), Y'(6, 2), Z'(2, 2)

PAGE 75—THE MIDPOINT FORMULA

1. $(\frac{1}{2}, 3)$ 2. $(2, -\frac{7}{2})$ 3. $(-\frac{9}{2}, 4)$ 4. $(1, -\frac{1}{2})$
5. $(\frac{5}{2}, \frac{3}{2})$ 6. $(\frac{5}{2}, 4)$ 7. (5, 6) 8. (6, 5)

PAGE 76—THE DISTANCE FORMULA

1. 5.39 2. 7.21 3. 9
4. 7.62 5. 7.07 6. 8.06